Pasta

Pasta

Sauces and Fillings for All Shapes and Sizes

Constance Jones

Friedman/Fairfax Publishers

A FRIEDMAN/FAIRFAX BOOK

Copyright © 1993 by Michael Friedman Publishing Group, Inc.

ISBN 1-56799-020-7

Editor: Stephen Williams
Designer: Judy Morgan
Photography Editor: Ede Rothaus

Typeset by Mar + x Myles Graphics, Inc.
Color separations by Kwong Ming Graphicprint Co.
Printed and bound in Hong Kong by Leefung-Asco Printers Ltd.

For bulk purchases and special sales, please contact:
Friedman/Fairfax Publishers
15 West 26 Street
New York, NY 10010
(212)685-6610 FAX (212)685-1307

Dedication

*For my mother and her mother, who taught me the
pleasures and rewards of the kitchen.*

CONTENTS

© Michael Grand

© Michael Grand

© Felicia Martinez/PhotoEdit

FINDING THE PERFECT PASTA

Nothing is better for entertaining than pasta. It's the perfect party food. The ancient Greeks and Romans knew this, and often served pasta at celebrations. Today no party-goer can resist the appeal of colorful, festive noodle dishes. These versatile, easy-to-prepare foods meet the busy party-giver's practical need for simplicity, but what's more important is that pasta dishes are fun! Whether you are entertaining a few close friends or a large group, all of your guests will delight in a fresh, well-prepared pasta dish.

Pasta: Creating, Celebrating & Saucing! outlines the path to pasta perfection, both in the kitchen and at the table. The opening sections introduce pasta's international history, diverse forms and countless adaptations. Next you learn everything you need to know about making fresh noodles and creating a wide variety of filled pastas. A section on cooking and serving techniques follows, giving you recipes for a multitude of sauces. Before you're halfway through, you'll be able to dazzle dinner guests with fabulous pasta dishes. But read on. The book's remaining pages deliver 20 unique menu suggestions, complete with party tips and a special pasta recipe. These menus offer entertaining ideas to fit every occasion and budget.

1 *Pasta Primer*

THE WORLD OF PASTA

No one knows how long pasta has been a dietary staple, but it seems certain that it's among the world's most ancient foods. Historical records show that the Chinese developed noodles, called *mein,* at least as early as 5000 B.C., and that in antiquity Bulgarian travelers carried provisions in the form of dried dough that they grated into pots of boiling milk or water at mealtimes. In ancient Greece and Rome, cooks prepared early versions of *tagliatelle* known as *laganon* or *laganum,* while a continent away the Chinese introduced noodles to Japan via Korea. At about the same time, the Arab world invented its own version of pasta, *couscous.*

Legend has it that Marco Polo first brought pasta to Europe, but the truth is that pasta had become a popular dish throughout Europe, Asia, the Middle East and North Africa, by the middle ages. Polo, who traveled to China in the late thirteenth century, may have been the first European to sample Asian noodles, but his fellow Italians were well acquainted with pasta long before he brought the delicacy back from the court of Kubla Khan. Five hundred years later, another traveler, an American named Thomas Jefferson, earned his place in culinary history when he visited Naples, Italy, and had four crates of "maccarony" shipped to the New World. A half-century later, an Italian immigrant opened the first American pasta factory, in Brooklyn, New York. Within a hundred years of that first factory, other noodle-loving immigrants from all over the world had guaranteed pasta a permanent place in the American diet.

In Italian, *pasta* means "paste." And that's exactly what it is, a pasty mixture of ground grain and liquid. But its infinite diversity of forms belies this simple description. For example, hard durum wheat semolina, a glutinous flour that makes a stiff dough, can be mixed with water to produce couscous and the many versions of dried Italian pasta. In fresh Italian pasta, a combination of eggs and bread flour yields golden noodles. Asians use bleached and whole-wheat flours as

© Burke/Triolo

Pasta has taken many forms over the years, including the mein *of the ancient Chinese, and the simple dried dough Bulgarian travelers grated into boiling water centuries ago. Here are some more modern— and quite delicious—pasta dishes:* (clockwise from top left) *tortellini with pesto; fusilli with vegetables; and linguini with shrimp and snow peas.*

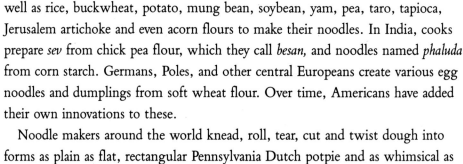

well as rice, buckwheat, potato, mung bean, soybean, yam, pea, taro, tapioca, Jerusalem artichoke and even acorn flours to make their noodles. In India, cooks prepare *sev* from chick pea flour, which they call *besan,* and noodles named *phaluda* from corn starch. Germans, Poles, and other central Europeans create various egg noodles and dumplings from soft wheat flour. Over time, Americans have added their own innovations to these.

Noodle makers around the world knead, roll, tear, cut and twist dough into forms as plain as flat, rectangular Pennsylvania Dutch potpie and as whimsical as cartwheel-shaped Italian *ruote.* Some flavor their dough with pureed vegetables, exotic spices and even chocolate. Others choose to boil, steam, poach, bake or fry their creations and serve them either hot or cold. Noodles can be stuffed and layered with meat, fish, fowl, vegetables, cheese and herbs. The choice of toppings includes sweet or savory sauces of every imaginable description, including plain butter, pureed frog's legs, sesame sauce and squid ink. All these variations only begin to tap the unlimited potential of this deceptively simple food.

Eating delectable pasta isn't just a sensual experience. Despite the common belief that pasta is just a delicious ethnic junk food, it's really very nutritious— and it definitely doesn't have to be fattening. Pasta is bulky, so it fills you up quickly without loading you down with calories. Two ounces of dried pasta cooked up into a 1-cup (about 5-ounce) serving, for instance, contains just over 200 calories, compared with 550 for five ounces of steak.

High in complex carbohydrates and low in fat, a typical serving of pasta offers 10 to 30 percent of the minimum daily requirements of several important vitamins and minerals. It also provides a surprising amount of protein: Ordinary dried pasta contains almost 10 grams of protein in a 1-cup serving, while "high-protein" pasta has about 15 grams. Whole-wheat pasta, meanwhile, also has dietary fiber. So, choose pasta—noodles, mein and couscous—for your body *and* your tastebuds.

© Michael Grand

There is a tremendous variety of dried pasta available for you to try. Some are ridged, some are curved and others evoke seashells on the beach. Whatever your tastes, there is sure to be a dried pasta shape that will please you. And the shapes aren't just for your eyes; they please the tastebuds too, because different shapes have different textures—and some are better suited than others for certain sauces.

Varieties of Dried Pasta

For generations, Americans have bought and served dried noodles and Italian-style pasta, mostly in the form of spaghetti, macaroni or egg noodles. Not only is this food inexpensive, filling and quick and easy to prepare, it also keeps almost indefinitely if stored in a cool, dry place. In recent years, commercial pasta makers have expanded their product lines with different shapes of pasta, and pasta tinted with spinach, carrots, tomatoes and other natural colorings. The available selection also includes Asian noodles and ready-made couscous. And because so many Americans are becoming health-conscious, some traditional Italian pasta shapes are now made with nutritious whole wheat, Jerusalem artichoke, corn and high-protein soy flour.

ITALIAN PASTA

Whether imported from Italy or manufactured in the United States, Italian-style dried pasta, *pasta secca,* should always be made with durum wheat flour or semolina (a more coarsely ground flour). Durum wheat is high in gluten, the substance that makes dough cohesive and elastic. When combined with water it yields a firm, easily shaped dough. Noodles made from this dough have a pleasing wheat flavor and are firm, not mushy. And they remain firm whether they are boiled or baked.

The astonishing array of pasta shapes that are available is due to the invention of a machine called the extruder. When fitted with the right die or mold, this machine turns dough into *linguine, penne,* or just about any other sort of noodle. Here's a list of the many varieties of dried Italian pasta available, categorized according to shape. With so many shapes to select from, you have almost unlimited choices when it comes to cooking with dried Italian pasta.

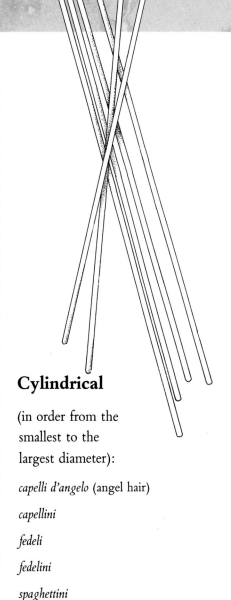

Cylindrical

(in order from the smallest to the largest diameter):

capelli d'angelo (angel hair)

capellini

fedeli

fedelini

spaghettini

spaghetti

vermicelli

Long tubes

(in order from the smallest to the largest diameter):

bucatini

fishietti

perciatelli

maccheroncini

maccheroni (macaroni)

mezza zita

zita (ziti)

zitone

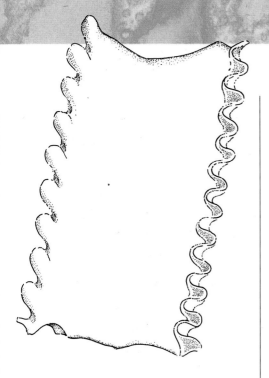

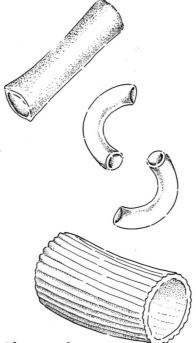

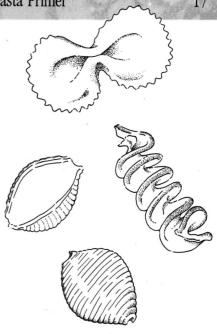

Flat

(in order from the narrowest to the widest):

lingue di passero

bavettine

linguine

bavette

tortiglioni (twisted into a spiral)

fusili (twisted into a spiral)

tagliolini

trenette or *reginelle*

mafalde (ripple-edged)

lasagnette (ripple-edged)

lasagne secche (ripple-edged)

Short tubes

(in order from the smallest to the largest diameter):

avelli

bombolotti

penne or *mostaccioli*

maltagliati

denti d'elefante (ribbed)

mezzi rigatoni (ribbed)

zita tagliati (zita cut short)

mille righi (ribbed elbow)

mille righi grandi (ribbed elbow)

rigatoni

cannelloni

manicotti rigati (grooved)

Fancy shapes

rotini, rotelle (spirals)

lumache (snail shells)

conchigli (sea shells)

conchigliette (small sea shells)

farfalle (butterflies)

fiochetti (small bows)

ditali (thimbles)

ruote (cartwheels)

stelline (little stars)

acine di pepe (peppercorns)

orzo (rice)

pastina

This cold noodle salad is evocative of many Asian pasta dishes. The bean sprouts, corn and mushrooms go well with a variety of noodles from the East.

ASIAN NOODLES

Although dried Asian noodles offer all of the diversity and delectability of Italian pasta, most Americans have until recently thought of them only in terms of lo mein or chow mein. Government regulations have done a lot to make Asian noodles mysterious. Because the United States Food and Drug Administration defines a noodle as something containing eggs, Asian manufacturers are required to give their non-egg noodles the unappetizing labels "alimentary paste" or "imitation noodles." People are often reluctant to try these mysterious products, but fortunately, a more appetizing label, "oriental noodles," is now becoming more common.

Almost all of the dried Asian noodles on the market are very high quality. You can buy egg and non-egg wheat noodles, rice noodles, bean threads and buckwheat noodles. Some of these come like spaghetti, in packages of separated, straight strips; others come in tangled cakes that dissolve into long noodles when boiled. The Chinese and Japanese varieties are the most familiar, but Burma, Cambodia, India, Indonesia, Korea, Laos, Malaysia, the Philippines, Singapore, Thailand and Vietnam all make their own noodles. Each of the Asian languages contains at least one general term for "noodle" that every pasta cook should know:

Burmese: *moh*

Chinese: *mian* (Mandarin) or *mein* (Cantonese)

Filipino: *pancit*

Indian: *sevian*

Indonesian, Malaysian, and Singaporean: *mee, mi*

Japanese: *men, menrui*

Korean: *gougsou*

Thai: *mee*

Here are basic types of dried Asian noodles that are widely available, their most familiar names, and their country of origin.

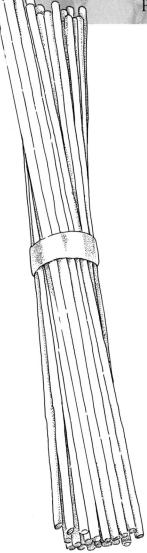

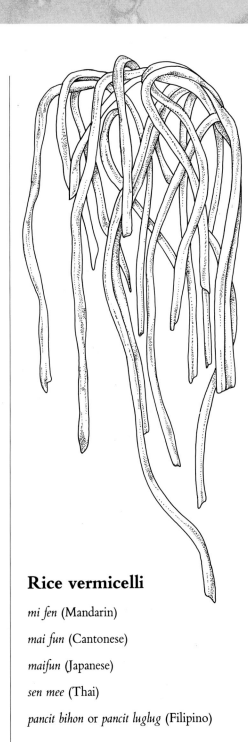

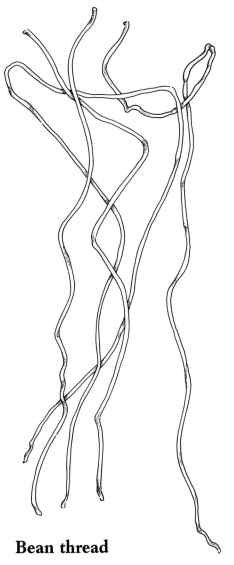

Non-egg wheat noodle

gan mian (Mandarin)

somen, udon, ramen (Japanese)

mee (Thai)

miswa (Filipino)

Rice vermicelli

mi fen (Mandarin)

mai fun (Cantonese)

maifun (Japanese)

sen mee (Thai)

pancit bihon or *pancit luglug* (Filipino)

Bean thread

(also called cellophane noodle, glass noodle, transparent noodle, shining noodle, or silver thread):

fun sie (Cantonese)

saifun, harusame (Japanese)

dang myun (Korean)

sotanghon (Filipino)

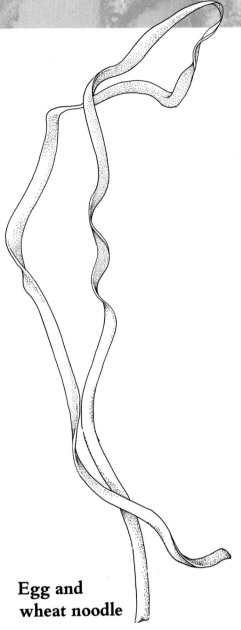

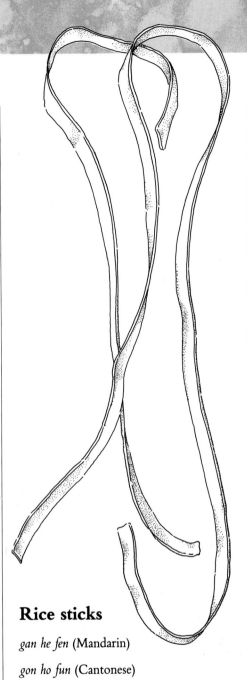

Egg and
wheat noodle

dan mian (Mandarin)

don mein (Cantonese)

Rice sticks

gan he fen (Mandarin)

gon ho fun (Cantonese)

Buckwheat noodle

soba (Japanese)

Fresh Pasta

Pasta lovers can find a wide variety of fresh noodles, both Italian and Asian, in specialty food stores and, increasingly, in supermarkets. Refrigerated wheat and rice noodles from China and Japan and ready-made *fettucine, tagliatelle*, and other Italian varieties offer a convenient alternative to dried pasta and fresh noodles. But while many of these noodles taste good, some are inferior to dried varieties, and none of them compare to the more time-consuming homemade pasta.

At first glance, making fresh pasta may appear to be a difficult task, but with the right equipment and a little practice it can be simple, enjoyable and rewarding. If you have a large, smooth marble or wood work surface, a rolling pin—preferably long, thin, and shaped like a short broomstick—and a very sharp knife, you have all the tools you need to make pasta by hand. An electric mixer or food processor speeds dough production, and an electric or manual pasta machine makes rolling and cutting the dough easy. Some electric machines, however, take almost all the work—and the fun—out of making pasta. They do every task, from mixing the dough to extruding the noodles, automatically. All you do is put the ingredients into the machine and flick a switch.

Durum semolina flour yields such a stiff dough that most people find it too difficult to use for homemade pasta. It can also clog electric machines. A combination of bread flour and eggs, called *pasta all'uovo* in Italian, yields the ideal dough for home pasta production. The fresh, flat noodles traditionally made from this dough include the narrow *tagliarini* (also called *tagliolini*), the slightly wider *tagliatelle* and medium-width *fettucine*, the even wider *pappardelle*, and the broadest of flat noodles, *lasagne*. The same dough goes into the various handmade fancy shapes such as *farfalle* and *orecchiette* (mushroom caps), as well as into the many stuffed pastas described in the next section. You can use whole-wheat, buckwheat, potato, and rice flours to make Italian, central European and Asian varieties; you can make doughs with water in place of eggs; and you can tint your noodles with vegetable juices, spices, or herbs. All of them are fun and easy to make and wonderful to eat.

These fresh, uncooked flat noodles have a rugged look that hides the exquisitely delicate texture of freshly-cooked pasta. Once they're cooked, they stimulate the appetite with their subtle aroma and inviting appearance. Add a sauce or filling and they're irresistible.

The Basics of Making Fresh Pasta

Pasta purists insist that handmade noodles have the best texture and flavor. But pasta machines produce thinner sheets of dough than anything the ordinary cook can roll by hand (they also come in handy during the kneading process) so they are a worthy addition to any kitchen arsenal. The only real problem with using pasta machines is that they are difficult to clean.

The typical pasta machine has three sets of rollers: a smooth set for rolling out dough into progressively thinner sheets; and two other sets grooved to cut the sheets of dough into narrow or wide noodles. Using a manual machine requires detaching and moving a single handle between the sets of rollers, depending on which set is being used. Electric machines require installation of a different set of rollers for each step of the process.

Manual and electric pasta makers differ in their advantages and disadvantages. Manually operated machines are cheaper than electrics, they permit finer control over how fast the dough passes through the rollers and they allow you to roll wider sheets of dough. But they also require more muscle power and dexterity. Electric machines work faster and free your hands to manipulate the dough, but they make a loud racket. Fully automatic electric pasta makers offer ultimate convenience, but limit creativity. They simply accept ingredients and deliver pasta five minutes later. All of these machines, though, do their jobs quite well.

Whereas dried pasta should only be made from hard wheat durum semolina, fresh pasta should be made from high-quality bread flour or unbleached all-purpose flour. Never use bleached flour, cake flour or self-rising flour, or the result will be unusable. For the best results, use only the freshest eggs: They lend pasta all'uovo the delicate flavor that distinguishes it from pasta secca. These ingredients are most often combined in the proportions of 1 large egg to a little more than 3/4 of a cup of flour. You may have to adjust your recipe to adapt to the climate and your ingredients. It's best to start with a little less flour and add more during the mixing process if the dough is too wet, because working extra liquid into dry dough is very difficult. A dash of salt heightens the flavor, and a few drops of olive oil will make the dough more manageable.

The five steps of the pasta-making process are mixing, resting, rolling, cutting and drying. Kneading plays the leading role in mixing the dough. When you knead, you encourage the gluten network in the dough to develop, giving the dough the elasticity it needs to stand up to rolling, cutting and, ultimately, cooking. After mixing the dough or rolling it out into sheets, you give it a rest to allow the gluten network to relax. This keeps the dough from becoming unmanageably stiff. When you roll the dough you should get sheets of dough thin enough to be translucent. Cut the dough with precision. Dry your pasta thoroughly if you don't plan to cook it right away.

A good pasta machine can be well worth the investment, because it will save you time, and give you more control over the thickness of your pasta. Plus, the machines are fun to use!

© Michael Grand

HOW TO MIX FRESH PASTA DOUGH

The following basic recipe produces approximately one pound of fresh pasta, enough to feed 4 to 6 people as a main course and 6 to 8 people as an appetizer or side dish. You can mix it by hand, with a food processor, or with an electric mixer. Use a pasta machine to help with the kneading, if you wish.

Classic Pasta all'uovo

3 cups bread flour

4 eggs

1 teaspoon salt (optional)

1 tablespoon olive oil (optional)

By hand:

1. Sift the flour into a heap on a flat, smooth work surface. Hollow out a well in the top so the mound resembles a volcano.

2. Crack the eggs into the well and add the salt and oil if desired. Beat the egg mixture with a fork or your fingers, gradually combining it with the surrounding flour. To do this, support the outer walls of the mound with one hand while pushing flour from the edge of the well into the egg mixture with the other. Continue until all of the flour and egg has been incorporated into a thick paste.

3. On a floured surface, knead the dough with the heel of your hand, adding more flour if the dough is sticky. The dough should be stiffer than bread dough. Knead for 5 to 10 minutes, until the dough is silky, smooth and elastic throughout.

With a food processor:

1. Into the bowl of your food processor put the flour and salt (if desired). Using a steel blade, process the dry ingredients for a few seconds to combine them.

2. Mix the eggs with a little olive oil in a measuring cup. The oil will help your machine process the dough more easily.

3. With the machine running, gradually pour the liquid ingredients through the feeding tube into the dry ingredients. Allow the processor to run for about 15 seconds, until a ball of dough forms around the bowl's central rod. Turn the machine off, test the dough, and add more flour if it is too sticky.

4. Remove the dough from the bowl of the processor. On a floured surface, knead the dough for about 3 minutes to improve its consistency.

© Felicia Martinez/PhotoEdit

In an electric mixer:

1. Using the paddle attachment, combine the dry ingredients in the bowl of the mixer.

2. Add the eggs and oil (if desired) and turn on the mixer. Small bits of dough should form in about 30 seconds.

3. Remove the paddle and replace it with a dough hook. Mix the dough for about 5 minutes, adjusting for wetness.

4. Place the dough on a flat surface dusted with flour and knead for 5 to 10 minutes until smooth.

With a pasta machine:

1. Prepare the dough by hand, with a food processor, or in an electric mixer, until it is ready for kneading.

2. Adjust the smooth rollers of your pasta machine to their widest setting and dust them with flour.

3. A handful at a time, pass the dough between the rollers. Fold the flattened dough into thirds or halves, rotate it 90 degrees, and pass it through the rollers again. If the dough is too porous, flour it before rolling it again.

4. Repeat the process up to 10 times, until the dough is smooth and has no holes. Do not knead it any more than necessary. Follow steps 2, 3 and 4 for the remaining dough.

PUTTING THE DOUGH TO REST

After kneading the dough, form it into a ball and place it in a bowl, or flour and stack the thick strips produced by your pasta machine. Cover the dough with a clean dish towel or plastic wrap and allow it to rest. The dough must rest for 30 minutes to 2 hours before you roll it. A longer resting time gives the gluten in the dough more time to relax, making the dough softer and easier to roll out into sheets.

ROLLING THE DOUGH INTO SHEETS

By hand:

1. Dust a large, flat work surface (preferably marble or wood) with flour. Place a ball of dough about the size of an orange in the center. Flour your rolling pin.

2. Pressing away from your body more than down into the dough, roll the ball of dough into a circle. Begin each stroke from the center of the circle, turning the circle 90 degrees between strokes. When the circle is 6 or 8 inches in diameter, rotate it 180 degrees between rolls to coax the dough into a rectangular strip. After every few strokes, check to make sure the dough is not sticking to the surface.

3. When you have a sheet about 1/4 inch thick, pull the far end of the strip toward you over the rolling pin and roll some of the dough onto the pin. Then roll and stretch the strip away from you and let it slide off the top of the pin.

4. While rolling, slide your hands evenly along the entire length of the rolling pin. This broad pressure will ensure that each stroke widens as well as lengthens the strip of dough.

5. Continue rolling and stretching until the strip is so thin you can see the grain of your wood or marble work surface through the dough. Then set the finished strip aside under a cloth.

6. Repeat the rolling process for the rest of your dough, loosely stacking the floured sheets under the cloth as you finish them. Let the sheets rest for about 15 minutes.

With a pasta machine:

1. If you have not already formed your dough into thick sheets by kneading it with your machine, set the smooth rollers to their widest opening, flour them, and run the dough through, a handful at a time, 3 or 4 times each.

2. Adjust the rollers to their second-widest setting, flour them, and run each sheet through once, lengthwise, without folding.

3. Repeat the rolling process once at each progressively narrower setting of the pasta machine. The sheets of dough should retain a uniform width, growing longer with each pass through the machine. Support the strips of dough and feed them into the machine with one hand while your other hand operates the rollers. Stop the machine periodically and slide the most recently rolled portion of the sheet out flat onto the work surface. Do not allow the rolled dough to bunch up as it comes out of the machine. If the sheets become too long to handle easily, cut them to more manageable lengths.

4. The finished sheets of pasta dough should be paper-thin and 12 to 18 inches long. Flour, stack, and cover the sheets and allow them to rest for 15 minutes.

Courtesy Williams-Sonoma

This electric pasta machine has attachments for rolling flat sheets of dough or making various types of noodles.

Courtesy DeFrancisci Machine Corp.

CUTTING NOODLES

By hand, for tagliarini (tagliolini), tagliatelle, fettuccine and pappardelle:

1. Using a very sharp knife and working on a wooden surface (Note: Never use a marble surface as a cutting board—if necessary, transfer the dough to a wooden surface), cut the sheets of dough into strips about 6 inches wide and 12 to 18 inches long. If the strips are sticky, sprinkle them with flour or cornmeal.

2. Fold the strips into loose, flat rolls 3 or 4 inches in diameter. You can do this in one of several ways: Roll each strip loosely from one end to the other, leaving half an inch or so unrolled at the end; fold the dough into an accordian-style stack; or fold the sheet inward from both ends of the strip simultaneously, until the 2 rolls almost meet in the middle.

3. Cut the rolled up strips into segments of the desired width:

1/8 inch for tagliarini
(or tagliolini)

1/4 inch for tagliatelle

1/3 inch for fettuccine

3/4 inch for pappardelle

When cutting, simply line your knife up carefully and press straight down. Do not use a slicing or sawing motion.

4. Pick up each noodle by its loose end to unroll it. If you folded the dough from both ends, slip your knife under the cut pasta sheet where the rolls meet in the middle and lift the knife to unroll all the noodles at once. Pile the noodles loosely and let them rest for 5 to 10 minutes before cooking.

By hand, for lasagne, farfalle and other fancy shapes:

1. For lasagne, cut the sheets of dough into 3-by-6-inch rectangles.

2. For farfalle, use a fluted pastry wheel to cut the sheets into 1-by-2-inch rectangles. Pinch each rectangle together at the center of its 2-inch length.

3. Only your imagination limits the different shapes you can create with pasta all'uovo. You can cut, twist, and pinch sheets of dough into any form you desire, or omit rolling altogether. Use your hands or any other kitchen tools to work pasta dough into tiny dumplings, orrechiette (mushroom caps) or any of an endless variety of festive shapes.

4. Pile the noodles loosely and let them rest for 5 to 10 minutes before cooking.

By machine, for tagliarini (tagliolini) and tagliatelle:

1. Use the narrow-grooved rollers for tagliarini/tagliolini; the wider-grooved set for tagliatelle. Flour the rollers.

2. The sheets of dough that you feed through the cutting rollers should be regularly shaped rectangles 12 to 18 inches long and no wider than your pasta machine's rollers.

3. With one hand as support, feed each sheet into the machine as you crank the rollers with the other hand. Stop the rollers frequently to spread the cut noodles out from the machine onto the work surface.

4. After cutting each sheet, clear the finished noodles from the machine and out of the way. Set the pasta aside for a few minutes before cooking.

DRYING AND STORING FRESH PASTA

Drying:

You can dry your pasta all'uovo for long-term storage by hanging it on a pasta rack, a clothesline, a towel rack, or even over the back of a chair for about 4 hours (depending on how humid your kitchen is). You can also dry your noodles on a towel in a loose heap, or wrap bunches of noodles around your hands to form loose nests and set them on a clean cloth to dry. Place it in a metal, plastic, or glass container with a tight-fitting top and store it in a cool, dry pantry or cabinet. It will keep indefinitely.

In the refrigerator:

If you intend to use your fresh pasta within a week of making it, place it loosely in an airtight container before it dries, and refrigerate.

In the freezer:

You may keep fresh, undried pasta frozen in an airtight container for up to a month.

© Michael Grand

Making and drying pasta is a very satisfying experience that leaves your kitchen filled with the aroma of fresh noodles. The drying pasta has a sculptural quality that hints at how beautiful the pasta dish you're preparing will be.

Varieties of Fresh Pasta

By adding extra ingredients to the basic pasta all'uovo recipe (page 26), you can create a wide range of delectable noodles. Here are a few popular recipes, each of which yields about a pound of fresh pasta.

© Michael Grand

You can make fresh pasta in brilliant colors by adding carrots, spinach, peppers, beets, herbs or other foods—one popular and dramatic pasta is even made jet black with squid ink. And fresh pasta can be formed into a variety of interesting shapes, as you can see in the photograph at left.

Buckwheat Pasta

Strongly flavored, with a hint of nuttiness, this pasta goes especially well with fresh green vegetables. The dough is fragile, so handle gently.

1¹/₂ cups buckwheat flour

1. Substitute the buckwheat flour for the same amount of bread flour in the standard pasta all'uovo recipe. Set aside ¹/₂ cup of the remaining bread flour to be added as necessary.

2. Combine the flour and eggs, adding the extra flour if you need it.

3. Prepare the pasta as described in the preceding section.

Note: To make eggless Japanese buckwheat noodles, or *soba,* substitute about 1¹/₄ cups of water for the eggs. Cut the noodles as thin as possible using a pasta machine or a sharp knife.

© Michael Grand

Tomato Pasta

Tomatoes lend a bright orange hue to pasta, a perfect complement to white sauces.

4 tablespoons tomato paste

1. Omit 1 egg from the standard recipe and add the tomato paste to the flour with the remaining eggs.

2. Prepare the pasta as described in the preceding section.

Saffron Pasta

Just a dash of saffron gives pasta a warm yellow glow. These noodles are especially lovely when served with red or green vegetables. Simply sift a pinch or two of saffron into the flour before combining it with the other ingredients, and prepare the pasta as described in the preceding section.

Whole-Wheat Pasta

These brown noodles have a hearty flavor and chewy texture that make them ideal for bold, spicy sauces. Follow the ingredients and directions for the classic pasta all'uovo, but substitute the following for the bread flour:

2 cups whole-wheat flour

1. Substitute the whole-wheat flour for the same amount of bread flour in the standard fresh pasta recipe, but set 1/2 cup of bread flour aside.

2. Mix the dry and wet ingredients, slowly adding the reserved flour if the dough is too sticky.

3. Prepare the pasta as described in the preceding section.

Semolina Pasta

Dough made from durum wheat semolina is hard to handle, but if you have plenty of muscle and energy, you might give this classic recipe a try.

3 cups semolina

1 teaspoon salt

1 cup water

4 tablespoons olive oil

1. Combine the semolina with the salt.

2. Mix the water and oil in a measuring cup.

3. Slowly add the water-oil mixture to the dry ingredients, mixing in thoroughly, a bit at a time. Keep the liquid well blended, and use only as much as necessary to make a damp but not sticky dough.

4. Prepare the pasta as described in the preceding section.

© Michael Grand

Herb Pasta

These delightful speckled noodles add extra zest to your favorite pasta dishes.

6 tablespoons fresh herbs or pesto

1. Prepare this recipe only with fresh herbs. You can use basil, coriander, dill, marjoram, oregano, parsley, sage, tarragon, thyme, or a combination of seasonings. Chop the herbs finely and mash in a mortar.

2. Add the herbs or pesto to the classic pasta all'uovo recipe along with the eggs.

3. Prepare the pasta as described in the preceding section.

Beet Pasta

Without changing the flavor of the pasta, beets give it a brilliant scarlet tint. For fun, combine these with white, green, or yellow noodles.

2 small, unpeeled beets, or 1 can cooked beets

1. If you are using fresh beets, boil them for 45 minutes to an hour, until tender.

2. Peel and chop the beets. Puree in a blender, food processor, or food mill.

3. Add 4 or more tablespoons of the beet puree to the flour, depending on how dark you want the pasta to be, along with 3 eggs.

4. Prepare the pasta as described in the preceding section.

Chili Pasta

To enliven pasta dishes made with meat or tomato sauces, try this peppery variation.

2 teaspoons cayenne pepper

1 tablespoon hot chili oil

1. Add the pepper and oil to the flour with the eggs.

2. Prepare the pasta as described in the preceding section.

Eggless Pasta

Most of the world's pasta types do not contain eggs, and here is a good example of a basic eggless recipe. If you need to avoid cholesterol, these noodles offer a healthy and tasty alternative.

3 cups bread flour

3/4 cup water

5 tablespoons olive oil

1. Add the olive oil to the dry ingredients as you would the eggs in pasta all'uovo. Blend for a few seconds.

2. Add the water to the paste and continue mixing.

3. Prepare the pasta as described in the preceding section.

Extra-Egg Pasta

Rich and golden, this pasta contains only the yolks of the extra eggs. The mouthwatering flavor of these noodles justifies the added cholesterol.

6 egg yolks

1. Substitute the egg yolks for 2 of the eggs in the standard recipe.

2. Prepare the pasta as described in the preceding section.

Spinach Pasta

This recipe yields the rich green noodles that have become a requisite in every pasta chef's repertoire.

1/2 pound fresh spinach

1. Cook the spinach in a very small amount of boiling water for 5 to 10 minutes, until tender.

2. Drain, rinse and pat the spinach dry, then puree it in a food processor, blender or food mill.

3. Omit 1 egg from the classic pasta all'uovo recipe and add the spinach puree to the flour along with the remaining eggs.

4. Prepare the pasta as described in the preceding section.

© Steven Mark Needham/Envision

*These delicious and chewy noo-
dles are a favorite in Japan,
where they're sold in noodle
shops in every neighborhood.
Combined with broth and seafood, meat or vegetables, they
make a wonderful and filling
soup.*

Japanese Udon

These thick, white, chewy noodles are a Japanese favorite, used most often in soup. Some cooks recommend wrapping the stiff dough in plastic and kneading it with your feet.

1 teaspoon salt

3 cups bread flour

1 cup water

1. Mix the salt into the bread flour.

2. Add about $2/3$ cup of the water to the dry ingredients and mix. If the dough does not cohere into a ball, add more water until it does.

3. Knead the dough for 10 minutes and allow it to rest for about an hour.

4. Roll the dough into sheets about $1/8$ inch thick.

5. Cut the sheets of dough into $1/4$-inch-wide noodles.

Chinese Egg Noodles

Not only can you use this recipe to make noodles that are great in Asian dishes, you can also cut the dough into 3-inch-square won tons or 7-inch-square egg roll wrappers.

3 cups bread flour

1 teaspoon salt

2 eggs

$1/2$ cup water

$1/4$ teaspoon sesame oil

1. Combine the salt and the flour.

2. Add the eggs and water to the dry ingredients and mix.

3. After kneading the dough, form it into a ball and smooth the sesame oil over its surface. Allow the dough to rest for about an hour.

4. Roll out the dough into sheets $1/16$ to $1/8$ inch thick, depending on how fat you like your noodles.

5. Cut the noodles $1/16$ to $1/8$ inch wide, and about 8 or 10 inches long.

Note: For an interesting oriental twist, flavor Chinese egg noodles with sesame paste, crushed ginger or chili pepper pulp. Add about 3 tablespoons of seasoning with the eggs, and slightly reduce the amount of water used. One-half cup of chopped fresh coriander added to the dough can also enhance the flavor of these noodles.

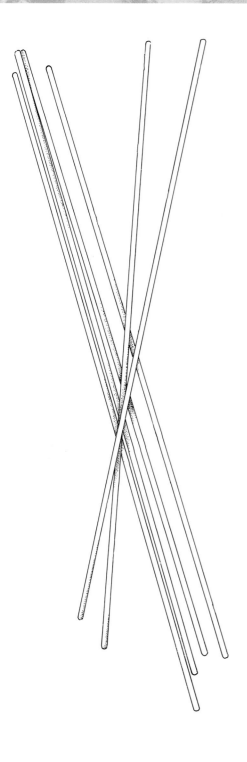

With these recipes at your command, you can create an almost infinite array of noodles. Once you get the hang of making pasta, experiment with your own ideas: Add chopped herbs to tomato pasta; black pepper to saffron noodles; chopped seaweed to udon; or seasonings such as curry powder, nutmeg or grated cheese to plain pasta all'uovo. You can even add unsweetened cocoa powder to your pasta to produce dark noodles that marry well with both sweet and savory sauces. Whatever your culinary inspiration, you're bound to have fun!

If you're entertaining guests or just preparing a meal for your family, pasta, stuffings and sauces can be combined to make perfect dishes that will be remembered long after the meal is over. You can make a tremendous variety of pasta dishes with the pastas and shapes described in this book. Just cook the pasta, fill it if you want and sauce it, using the recipes that follow as your guides.

While almost everyone is familiar with the classic Italian pasta dishes, like stuffed cannelloni, spaghetti with meat sauce, and lasagne, there are many wonderful pasta dishes from other countries, too. Try pierogi, from Eastern Europe, or won tons from China. And sauces aren't limited to tomato and meat sauces. You can make interesting sauces from vegetables, fish and other ingredients.

There are enough great recipes here to satisfy anyone for a long time, but don't limit yourself. The secret to making great pasta dishes is to use the guidelines given here, and then let your imagination help you create exactly the meals you desire. Pasta is a versatile food, and you'll find that it goes well with a wide range of stuffings and sauces.

One of the most enticing pasta dishes you can make includes ripe olives, tuna and fresh peppers in a pesto sauce. Add your own favorite ingredients if you like.

2 Pasta Fillings

STUFFED PASTA

Filled pastas are among the most exciting pastas, because they offer an incredible array of tastes and textures that take the pasta experience far beyond simple spaghetti and meatballs. Some filled pastas are more easy to prepare than others, but with such a wide selection to choose from, you're certain to find a variety that will fit your time and budget constraints.

Of course, the easiest dinners to prepare are those that are made by someone else—and you can find a number of ready-made stuffed pastas at most grocery stores. However, not all of them are equally good. The highest quality store-bought varieties are the fresh, refrigerated tortellini, ravioli, won tons, and pierogi that are widely available. Frozen versions of the same pasta are second best. Dried stuffed pastas are not as good as either frozen or fresh, but you can still experiment with them. Unfortunately, the frozen and the dried varieties are sometimes bland and heavy, so it's best to use them only when you can't buy fresh pasta.

Of course, the best method of all is to make your own. The basic dough recipes are the same as for other pastas, and the fillings aren't difficult to make. In no time at all you'll be experimenting with your own combinations. Be assured that once you try making your own filled pasta, you will wonder why you ever bothered to buy it at the store. Whoever you serve your homemade stuffed shapes to will be very impressed.

Filled pastas give you an incredible variety of textures, shapes and colors to choose from. You can buy frozen or dried filled pasta, but fortunately most types are easy enough to prepare at home. And they taste better if you make them yourself. However you prepare them, filled pastas offer you the chance to serve anything from a simple, country meal to an elegant and sophisticated dinner.

The Classic Shapes

One of the most wonderful things you can do with pasta is cut sheets of it into squares, rectangles or circles and fold these shapes into little packages stuffed with succulent filling. Stuffed pasta, *pasta ripiena* in Italian, combines the delicate taste and texture of pasta with savoury fillings that are a special treat for the tastebuds. And the pleasures of this type of dish extend far beyond the familiar appeal of ravioli. From *agnolotti* to *ziti,* from *pierogi* to *won tons,* filled pasta offers an array of international culinary possibilities to the imaginative cook.

Filled pasta can assume almost any form and you can invent all kinds of ways to fold pasta packets around luscious fillings. Feel free to try any stuffing: Goat, Gruyère, or ricotta cheeses; pumpkin, eggplant, or sun-dried tomatoes; sweetbreads, prosciutto, or curried chicken; red snapper, king crab, or Maine lobster.

© Burke/Triolo

Stuffed shells never go out of style. These jumbo shells have been filled with a delicious combination of chicken and vegetables in a light curry sauce. The beauty of stuffed shells is that you can fill them with almost anything you wish. There aren't any hard and fast rules when it comes to making delicious stuffed pasta dishes.

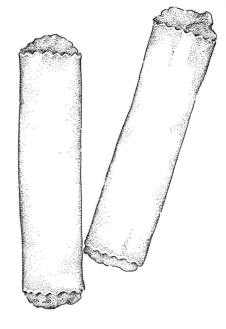

ITALIAN STUFFED SHAPES

The Italians have perfected the art of stuffing pasta, and their creativity seems to have no limits. Everyone is familiar with ravioli and manicotti, but there is a tremendous variety of Italian pastas beyond these shapes. You don't have to limit yourself when stuffing Italian pasta. Let your imagination wander, and choose your pasta from among the wonderful varieties in this list.

Squares

Agnolotti: squares of pasta all'uovo with a meat or vegetable filling sandwiched between them; also referred to as *ravioli*

Pansooti: like *ravioli* but larger

Ravioli: like *agnolotti* but traditionally filled with ricotta cheese; now widely used as a generic term to describe both *ravioli* and *agnolotti*

Raviolini: like *ravioli* but smaller

Tubes

Cannelloni: rectangles of pasta all'uovo rolled into tubes and filled with meat or vegetables

Manicotti: like *cannelloni* but sealed at the ends

Rigatoni: large, ribbed pasta secca tubes filled with any stuffing

Rotoli: large sheets of pasta spread with filling and rolled like a jelly roll into long cylinders; sliced to serve

Ziti: medium-sized pasta secca tubes stuffed with any filling

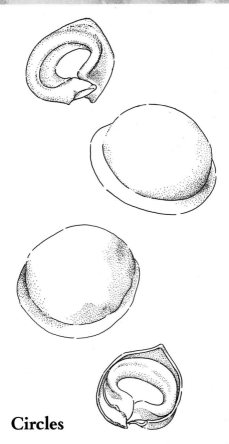

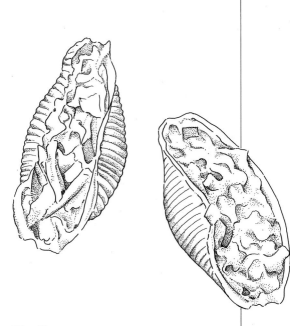

Circles

Cappelletti: circles of pasta all'uovo stuffed with a filling and formed to resemble a miter hat

Tortelletti: circles or squares of pasta all'uovo folded over a filling and sealed around the open edges

Tortelli: large circles or squares of pasta all'uovo with a filling sealed in between

Tortellini: circles of pasta all'uovo folded over a filling and bent to resemble a little doughnut

Tortelloni: like *tortellini* but larger

Shells

Conchigli: stuffed, seashell-shaped pasta secca

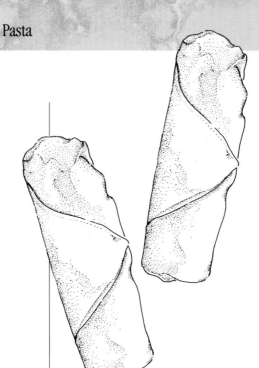

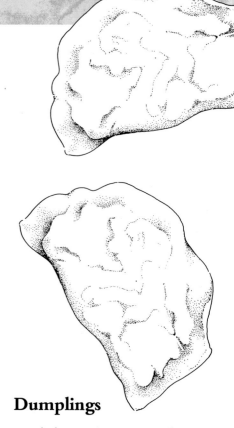

STUFFED PASTAS FROM OTHER COUNTRIES

The Italians aren't the only people who have developed various stuffed pastas. All cultures that use pasta have their unique stuffed pasta dishes. And for good reason. They're delicious, compact, and often quite simple to make. The following list will give you a good idea of the variety of stuffed pastas that are made around the world. Many of these are easy to make at home. And all of them are wonderful for serving to guests.

Asian Rolls and Dumplings

Egg rolls, or *lumpia* (Asian): egg-based rice or wheat wrappers filled with vegetables, and sometimes seafood rolled into cylindrical jackets and deep fried

Spring rolls (Vietnamese): rice paper filled with a combination of vegetables, meat, and seafood and rolled into cylindrical packets that are fried in oil

Won tons, potstickers, gyoza (Asian): egg-based or non-egg wheat or rice wrappers filled with seafood, meat, and vegetables, folded and sealed shut then fried, steamed or poached

Dumplings

Kreplach (Jewish): squares of egg-based wheat dough folded into triangles over meat or cheese stuffing that are boiled

Pierogi (Polish): circles of egg-and-wheat dough stuffed with potatoes, cheese, meat, or sauerkraut and folded shut then boiled

Vareniki (Ukranian): circles or squares of egg-and-wheat dough folded over a cottage cheese filling and sealed at the open edges that are boiled

Asian cooks use a variety of spices and cooking tools that might not be completely familiar to most cooks. But you can find everything you need, including the ingredients shown here, in a well-stocked supermarket or a store that specializes in Oriental food.

Making Filled Pasta

All you really need to make filled pasta is a sharp knife, a round cookie cutter and your fingers, but it won't hurt to purchase a few other helpful tools. For the cookie cutter you can substitute a special circular stamp with serrated edges, or you can cut rectangular shapes with a plain or fluted pastry wheel rather than with a knife. If you can't cut a straight line, mark your sheets of dough with perfect squares with a ravioli roller. An indented ravioli tray that looks like a tin for small, square muffins creates more possibilities. Lay a sheet of dough onto the tray, place filling in the hollows, lay a second sheet over the top and seal the squares with a few passes of a rolling pin to create ravioli. For gadget lovers, these items enhance the pleasure of cooking. Most cooks, however, easily construct their filled pasta without them.

For Italian shapes and other international shapes, the basic pasta all'uovo recipe given in the section on fresh pasta makes ideal wrappers. Store-bought dried cannelloni, rigatoni, shells and ziti can be partially cooked and then used like fresh pasta. And some cooks adapt parboiled lasagna secca to pasta ripiena dishes like cannelloni and manicotti. The Chinese egg noodle recipe found in the section on fresh pasta is a good basis for won ton or egg roll skins. You can also buy perfectly acceptable dried rice paper and fresh or frozen won ton or gyoza skins, rice noodle sheets and spring roll or lumpia wrappers for use in stuffed Asian pasta dishes. Some of the international recipes that follow require unique doughs not found in stores. In these cases, the recipes include instructions for making the traditional doughs.

With the exception of Asian dumplings, you should roll out the dough for stuffed pasta in sheets a bit thicker than when cutting noodles. The second-narrowest setting on a pasta machine's smooth rollers will produce a sheet of about the right thickness. Extra weight lends strength to the dough, so that you are less likely to tear it while filling, cooking, or serving your pasta. Another way to protect the pasta from damage is to cut and shape the dough as soon as possible after rolling it out. That keeps it from drying and becoming unmanageably brittle.

Fillings for the smaller shapes should be chopped very finely or pureed so that they easily fit into their wrappers and contain no tough chunks that can rip the pasta. Take care to drain fillings of excess juices before they come into contact with the pasta. Too-wet fillings weaken the dough by making it soggy. And many of the ingredients used to stuff pasta must be pre-cooked. The short cooking time for the pasta is insufficient to cook the stuffing thoroughly.

When you add your stuffing to the pasta, be sure to leave clean borders at least 1/4 inch deep around the edge of the dough. Grease and stuffing will keep the edges from sealing shut properly. Brush egg white onto the clean border to ensure a good seal.

For the freshest, most appetizing results, cook and serve the filled shapes immediately following a short rest period of 15 minutes to 1 hour. To make stuffed pasta in advance, get it ready on the same day you intend to cook it. Seal it in an airtight container and refrigerate it until you are ready to begin cooking. Stuffed pasta prepared and stored this way will keep for a few days, and if carefully wrapped and frozen, it will last about a month.

Making filled pasta requires patience and care, but it can also be gratifying, with delicious results.

© Burke/Triolo

Seafood and pesto are an intriguing combination for stuffed shells. Here the shells have been filled with a mixture of crabmeat, fresh herbs and diced green peppers in a light cream sauce. The presentation on a pesto sauce with fresh red and yellow peppers is almost irresistible.

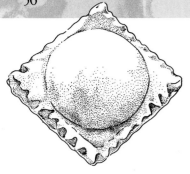

SPECIAL TECHNIQUES

Here are the techniques for forming the classic Italian shapes. You can stuff them with almost any filling.

Agnolotti, Pansooti, Ravioli and Raviolini

These 4 shapes only differ in size. Although purists insist ravioli only refers to pasta stuffed with ricotta cheese, most people use the name for any type of filled pasta square. You can cut and fill squares of any size. The dimensions given here are traditional but not mandatory.

1. Prepare about 1 pound of pasta all'uovo and roll it out into 2 rectangular sheets of approximately the same size.

2. A teaspoon at a time, place lumps of filling in rows on 1 sheet of the dough. For ravioli or agnolotti, position the mounds about 2 inches apart, with a 1-inch border along the edges of the sheet. To prepare raviolini, use 1/2-teaspoon lumps placed on the sheet of dough at 1-inch intervals; for pansooti, use 2-teaspoon lumps placed 3 inches apart.

3. Brush the exposed dough between the lumps with water or egg white.

4. Lay the second sheet of dough over the first, and press down around each mound of filling to seal the sheets together.

5. Use a knife or pastry wheel to form the individual ravioli. Cut straight down the center of the dough borders that separate the lumps of filling.

6. Allow the ravioli to rest for up to an hour, making sure that they do not touch each other, or they will stick.

7. Boil for 5 to 10 minutes, depending on the size of the ravioli. One pound of pasta dough yields enough ravioli to serve 4 to 6 people.

© Steven Mark Needham/Envision

An unusual ravioli made with beets is presented here resting in a bechamel sauce. This surprising dish is made even more special with a caviar garnish. This combination of flavors is a demonstration of the wonderful types of pasta you can devise if you let your imagination wander.

Cannelloni and Manicotti

These stuffed tubes are rolled slightly differently. Whereas cannelloni are open-ended tubes, the ends of manicotti are sealed shut. Cannelloni traditionally contained meat, and manicotti, a ricotta-based stuffing, but the old rules no longer apply. Cannelloni has now come to signify all forms of filled pasta all'uovo tubes. You can also buy preformed pasta secca tubes for use in cannelloni or manicotti.

1. Prepare about 1 pound of pasta all'uovo and roll it into a rectangular sheet.

2. For cannelloni, cut the pasta into 4-inch squares. For manicotti, cut 4-by-6-inch rectangles.
   A pound of dough should yield about 18 cannelloni wrappers and 12 manicotti wrappers.

3. Boil the pasta for 2 or 3 minutes in salted water. Drain in a colander and lay the pieces on a damp cloth to cool. Do not let the pieces touch, or they will stick together.

4. Lay a log of filling about 1 inch in diameter down the center of each rectangle (for manicotti, place the strip of filling parallel to the long sides of the wrapper). For cannelloni these logs should extend all the way to the edges of the squares. For manicotti they should end about 3/4 of an inch from the short edges.

5. Roll up the cannelloni into a simple filled pipe. For manicotti, flip the short edges inward and roll from one of the long edges to form a thin egg-roll shape.

6. Place the tubes in a pan, seams down. Add sauce, cheese, or other toppings and bake for 10 to 15 minutes at 350 degrees. Twelve manicotti or 18 cannelloni will serve up to 6 people.

Cappelletti

In Italian, *capelletti* means "little hats," and that is exactly what they look like.

1. Prepare about 1 pound of pasta all'uovo and roll it out into a sheet.

2. Brush about 1/3 of the sheet with beaten egg and cut smooth-edged circles 1 1/2 to 2 inches in diameter from the coated section.

3. Drop 1/2 teaspoon of filling into the center of each circle and fold the pasta over the stuffing to form a semicircle. Lightly press the edges together to seal them.

4. Grip each end of the semicircle's diameter—the straight, folded edge—between thumb and forefinger, bend the two ends of the diameter toward each other until they overlap slightly to form tubes, and pinch them together. The results should resemble a rounded version of a bishop's or a high priest's miter.

5. Repeat steps 2 through 4 for the remaining thirds of the pasta sheet.

6. Leaving a bit of space between them, set the cappelletti aside to rest for 15 to 60 minutes before cooking.

7. Cook by boiling about 5 minutes. This recipe serves 4 to 6 people.

© Burke/Triolo

This cannelloni presentation is breaking the traditional rules, which held that cannelloni was filled with meat, and manicotti was filled with cheese (manicotti is basically just cannelloni with the ends sealed shut after cooking). Some rules are made to be broken.

Rotoli

This simple recipe is considerably quicker than those for most filled pasta dishes. The pasta for rotoli should be rolled out a bit thicker than for other filled shapes, because otherwise the large sheets will tear while being handled. To ensure that the rolls cook evenly, poach them in simmering, not boiling, water.

1. Prepare about 1/2 pound of pasta all'uovo and roll half of it out into a 10-by-20-inch rectangle.

2. Spoon the filling onto the sheet and spread it evenly to a thickness of about 1/2 inch, leaving a border of pasta 1 inch wide around the edges of the rectangle.

3. Starting at one of the 10-inch edges, gently roll up the coated sheet as you would a jelly roll. Be careful not to squeeze any of the filling out the ends.

4. Brush a little water or egg white on the seam to form a seal, and press the ends of the roll shut to contain the filling.

5. Wrap the roll tightly in 3 or 4 layers of cheesecloth and tie the ends with string.

6. Roll out the rest of the pasta into a sheet and repeat steps 2 through 5.

7. Poach the rolls in simmering water for 30 to 40 minutes. To serve, remove the cheesecloth and slice the rolls with a knife dipped in hot water. This recipe will yield about 4 portions.

Tortellini and Tortelloni

An old Italian tale explains the colorful origin of this favorite pasta shape. According to the story, Venus, the Roman goddess of love, stopped one night at an inn in Bologna. Smitten by Venus' beauty, the proprietor decided to spy on her in her chambers. The poor innkeeper could see no more than the navel of the naked goddess through the keyhole. However, he was so inspired that he recreated the lovely vision of her navel in pasta.

1. Prepare about 1 pound of pasta all'uovo and roll it out into a sheet.

2. Cut the dough into 2-inch circles for tortellini, 3-inch circles for tortelloni.

3. Place 1 or 1 1/2 teaspoons of filling, depending on the size of the circles, into the center of each shape.

4. Fold each circle into a semicircle and pinch the edges together.

5. Bend the rounded border in toward the filled section of each semicircle, while bending the straight, folded edge in the opposite direction around your index finger. Press the pointed ends together.

6. Allow the finished shapes to rest for up to an hour. During this time, do not allow them to touch each other.

7. Cook in boiling water for 5 minutes. This recipe serves 4 to 6 people.

Tortellini is a very adaptable pasta that can be sauced and filled with a variety of flavors to complement the season or the occasion. This tortellini is filled with pumpkin and topped with a light curry sauce (see recipe, page 113). It's a delightful dish to serve with a green salad, alongside a centerpiece of autumn squash.

Tortelli

Tortelli are circles and squares that are 4 inches or larger. If you make them large enough, a single piece can serve as an entire first course or light entree.

1. Prepare about 1 pound of pasta all'uovo and roll it out into a sheet.

2. Cut 4-, 5- or 6-inch squares or circles from the dough.

3. Set half of the pieces aside and place a few tablespoons of filling on the others, leaving a 1/2-inch border of pasta around the edge of each.

4. Brush egg white or water on the borders and place the remaining pieces over the filled shapes. Press the edges together to seal them. Allow the tortelli to rest for 15 minutes to an hour, separated from each other so they will not stick together.

5. Cook the tortelli in rapidly boiling salted water for 2 to 5 minutes. Serves 4 to 6.

Tortelleti

These are similar to ravioli and tortelli, except that you cut the pasta shapes before filling them, and fold the stuffing into pockets rather than sandwiching it between 2 pieces of dough.

1. Prepare about 1 pound of pasta all'uovo and roll it out into a sheet.

2. Cut the dough into 2-inch squares or circles, and dab 1 teaspoon of filling into the center of each.

3. Brush the exposed pasta borders with egg white or water and fold the shapes in half over the filling.

4. Press the edges together to seal them. Allow the tortelleti to rest for at least 15 minutes, separated so they don't stick together.

5. Boil the tortelleti for about 8 minutes. A pound of pasta dough makes enough tortelleti to serve 4 to 6.

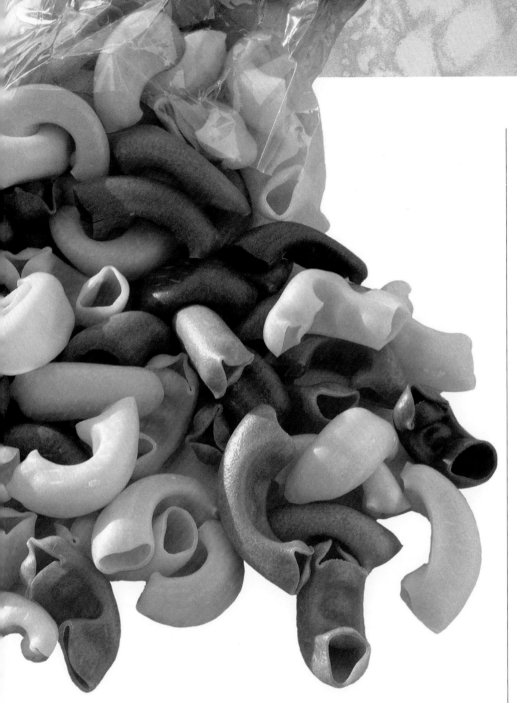

The Dried Shapes

By using dried pasta shapes, you can save time on certain filled pasta dishes.

1. Cook 1 pound of pasta secca conchigli, rigatoni, ziti, or cannelloni tubes in 1 gallon of boiling salted water for 8 to 15 minutes, depending on the shape. Cook the pasta al dente—flexible but firm.

2. Drain the pasta and rinse it thoroughly in cold water. Set it on a damp cloth, separating each piece from the others so they will not stick to each other.

3. When cool, fill the shapes using a spoon or your fingers and place them in a baking dish.

4. Cover the stuffed pasta with sauce and bake at 350 degrees for 25 to 30 minutes. Serves 6 to 8 people.

MAKING THE FILLINGS

All of these wonderful fillings will adapt to any pasta shape. You can enjoy a new combination every night for months.

Savory Cheese Filling

Cheese-filled pasta has long been a favorite, for good reason. It's rich yet light, and adapts well to all kinds of sauces, especially the much loved tomato-based varieties.

1 pound ricotta

1/2 cup shredded mozzarella

1/2 cup grated Parmesan cheese

1 egg

2 tablespoons fresh or 2 teaspoons dried chopped parsley

salt and pepper to taste

1. Combine all the ingredients in a bowl and mix well. Makes enough to fill pasta for 4 to 6 people.

Spinach and Cheese Filling

There are as many ways to prepare this colorful stuffing as there are cooks. Try making the basic recipe given here with mascarpone or cottage cheese, or substitute another green, such as chard, for the spinach.

1 pound spinach

1 cup ricotta

1 cup grated Parmesan cheese

1 large clove garlic, minced

1 egg

1/2 teaspoon nutmeg

salt and pepper to taste

1. Rinse the spinach. Using only the water left clinging to its leaves, cook it in a covered pot for five minutes or until tender.

2. Drain and chop the spinach into fine pieces.

3. Combine all of the ingredients in a bowl to form a thick paste. This will fill enough pasta for 4 to 6 people.

Ham and Cheese Filling

This mouth-watering recipe calls for prosciutto, an Italian specialty most often imported from the Italian city of Parma. Prosciutto is a ham cured without smoke and sliced paper-thin. It's frequently used in antipasto.

4 ounces prosciutto

1 cup ricotta

1/2 pound mozzarella, shredded

3 tablespoons grated Parmesan cheese

1 egg

1 tablespoon fresh or 1 teaspoon dried chopped parsley

salt and pepper to taste

1. Cut the prosciutto into pieces about 1/8 inch square.

2. Combine all the ingredients in a bowl and mix well. This recipe makes up to 6 servings.

© Burke/Triolo

Recipes for fillings can be reworked to suit the tastes of the cook and the guests. The spinach and cheese filling in these shells is always popular with guests, and there are numerous ways to prepare it. But it's hard to go wrong if you follow the basic recipe, and add any additional spices that you choose.

© Michael Grand

Classic Meat Filling

Traditional Italian meat fillings often incorporate mortadella, a mild pork sausage made in Bologna, with other meats. For this recipe, however, you can use whatever leftover meat you might have in your refrigerator.

1 small onion, chopped

30g (1 oz) melted butter

125g (4 oz) pork

60g (2 oz) uncooked chicken

125ml (4 fl oz) dry white wine

60g (2 oz) prosciutto

60g (2 oz) mortadella

1 egg

185g (6 oz) grated Parmesan cheese

1/4 teaspoon nutmeg

salt and pepper to taste

1. Sauté the onion in the melted butter until transparent.

2. Add the pork and chicken. Sear the meat for 2 minutes on each side, then lower the heat and add the wine. Cook, covered, for 10 minutes, until the meat is no longer pink.

3. While the pork and chicken cool, dice the prosciutto and mortadella as small as possible. Then finely dice the cooked pork and chicken, and mix all of the meats together in a bowl.

4. Process the meat in a food processor or blender until finely ground. For coarser cannelloni filling, skip this step.

5. Combine all the ingredients in a bowl and mix thoroughly. Makes enough for 4 to 6 people.

Veal Filling

If you are in the mood for pasta stuffed with meat, but want a filling that's not quite so hearty as the classic meat recipe, try this veal dish.

2 tablespoons olive oil

1 sprig thyme

2 bay leaves

2 sage leaves

1 small onion, chopped

250g (8 oz) veal

125g (4 oz) prosciutto

125ml (4 fl oz) dry white wine

250g (8 oz) spinach

salt and pepper to taste

2 eggs

1. Put the oil, thyme, bay, sage, and onion in a pan and cook until the onion is transparent.

2. Add the veal, prosciutto, and white wine. Cover and simmer for 45 minutes, until most of the liquid is gone.

3. Rinse the spinach and cook it in very little boiling water for 3 minutes. Drain and squeeze it dry, then chop it finely.

4. When the meat is cooked, remove the thyme, bay and sage leaves. Allow the meat to cool, then dice.

5. Mix the meat and spinach, then process to a paste in a food processor or blender if you plan to use the filling in any of the smaller shapes.

6. Add salt and pepper if desired, and mix in the eggs. Make sure the mixture is well blended before using it to stuff pasta. Serves 4 to 6.

© Michael Grand

Spicy Lamb Filling

This recipe offers a taste of the Middle East. Substitute mint and mustard for the dried spices, and you will enjoy a truly unusual dish.

2 tablespoons olive oil

1 medium onion, chopped

1 pound ground lamb

2 teaspoons curry powder

1 teaspoon cumin

1/2 teaspoon cayenne pepper

salt and pepper to taste

1. Cook the onions in the olive oil until clear.

2. Add the lamb and sauté it until it has lost its pinkness. Stir often so it does not form lumps.

3. Add the spices to the meat, lower the heat, and cover the pan. Cook for about 8 minutes.

4. If you are using this recipe to stuff cannelloni, proceed to step 5. Otherwise, process the meat mixture in a blender or food processor to make a fine paste. Add extra olive oil if necessary.

5. Fill pasta. Serves 4 to 6.

© Michael Grand

Chicken Filling

This blend of meat, mushrooms and spinach is excellent in stuffed pasta.

4 tablespoons butter

1 pound boneless chicken

1/2 pound mushrooms, chopped

1/2 onion, chopped

1/2 pound fresh spinach

1/4 cup light cream

2 eggs

1/4 teaspoon nutmeg

salt and pepper to taste

1. Sauté the chicken in 2 tablespoons of butter until it loses all pinkness. Allow the meat to cool, then dice it finely.

2. Cook the mushrooms and onions in the rest of the butter.

3. Rinse the spinach and parboil it for about 3 minutes, until tender. Drain and squeeze it dry, then chop it.

4. Combine all of the ingredients in a bowl. Use a food processor or blender if you want a paste. Fills enough pasta to serve 4 to 6 people.

© Steven Mark Needham/Envision

Fresh Fish Filling

This is a lovely way to serve the catch of the day.

500g (1 lb) fresh fish fillets

15g (1/2 oz) butter

125ml (4 fl oz) white wine

1 tablespoon olive oil

1 large clove garlic, chopped

pinch of thyme

pinch of marjoram

1 egg

60g (2 oz) grated Parmesan cheese

salt and pepper to taste

1. Sauté the fish quickly on both sides in butter. Add the wine and reduce the heat. Cook, covered, for 5 to 10 minutes.

2. Heat the olive oil and add the garlic, thyme and marjoram. Sauté until the garlic starts to brown, then remove from the heat.

3. Flake the fish in a bowl and add the herbed oil, egg and Parmesan cheese. Mix thoroughly and add salt and pepper if desired.

4. Fill the pasta. Serves 4 to 6 people.

Mushroom Filling

Stuffed pasta made with this rich filling is perfect for the most elegant dinners, yet simple enough to prepare on the spur of the moment. Add some finely chopped prosciutto for a delicious variation.

375g (12 oz) button mushrooms

60g (2 oz) butter

1 clove garlic, minced

60g (2 oz) ricotta

60g (2 oz) mascarpone or cream cheese

2 tablespoons fresh or 1 teaspoon dried chopped parsley

3 tablespoons grated Parmesan cheese

salt and pepper to taste

1. Rinse and dry the mushrooms. Chop them finely and sauté them in the butter with the garlic.

2. Combine all of the ingredients in a bowl and mix well. Makes enough to fill pasta for 4 to 6 people.

Aubergine Filling

As the nights cool down at the end of the summer and aubergine comes into season, the promise of this recipe's delectable results will coax you into the kitchen.

1 aubergine—about 375g (12 oz)

2 small courgettes

1/2 onion, chopped

3 tablespoons olive oil

375g (12 oz) tomato purée

salt and pepper to taste

1. Dice the aubergine. Soak the cubes in salted water for 30 minutes, then drain. Spread the aubergine on a flat surface and cover it with a plate or pan. Weight the pan with a book or a can so that any excess moisture is pressed out of the aubergine. Use a clean towel to pat the aubergine dry.

2. Chop the courgettes and onion. Heat the olive oil in a pan and add all of the vegetables. Sauté until tender.

3. Purée the vegetables in a blender or food processor.

4. Add tomato purée and seasonings and mix well. This recipe fills enough pasta to serve up to 6 people.

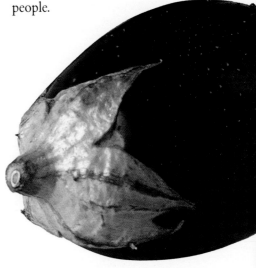

Among the most popular stuffed pastas are Asian rolls. The many varieties include these Chinese Egg Rolls, stuffed with shrimp, cabbage and red pepper. The garnish is Chinese parsley, also called cilantro and coriander.

© Guy Powers/Envision

STUFFED PASTAS FROM OTHER COUNTRIES

Stuffed pasta isn't just an Italian specialty. Dumplings, rolls, tubes and other shapes have been developed independently throughout the world. Cooks in Europe, Asia, the Middle East and the United States have devised numerous delicious variations on the theme of stuffed pasta.

Chinese Potstickers

Pork dumplings are a favorite all over Asia, especially when made using the potsticker technique. Serve potstickers with a dipping sauce of equal parts rice vinegar and soy sauce flavored with fresh ginger, garlic or hot spicy oil.

1/2 pound spinach or Chinese cabbage

2 teaspoons sesame oil

1 pound ground pork

1/4 cup chopped water chestnuts

2 scallions, minced

1 teaspoon fresh ginger, grated

1 tablespoon soy sauce

1 tablespoon corn starch

60 won ton skins (store-bought, or see Chinese egg noodle recipe, page 41)

4 tablespoons peanut oil

1 cup hot water

6 tablespoons sake (Japanese rice wine)

1. Clean, parboil, squeeze dry and chop the greens.

2. Heat the sesame oil in a wok. Add the pork, water chestnuts, scallions, ginger and soy sauce. Cook until the meat is done.

3. Allow the meat to cool, then mix in the corn starch and the greens.

4. Place a teaspoon of filling in the center of each won ton wrapper. Fold the wrapper into a triangle and seal the edges. Flip the ends of the folded edge in toward the center of the triangle, and press the two points together.

5. Heat 2 tablespoons of the peanut oil in a wok, coating the sides of the pan. Lay half of the won tons in the pan so that they all make contact with its surface. Cook at medium heat until they are lightly browned on the bottom, then add 1/2 cup of the hot water and 3 tablespoons of the sake. Reduce the heat and cook, uncovered, until all the liquid is gone.

6. Repeat step 5 for the remaining dumplings.

7. Serve as a main dish for 4 to 6, or as an appetizer for up to 12.

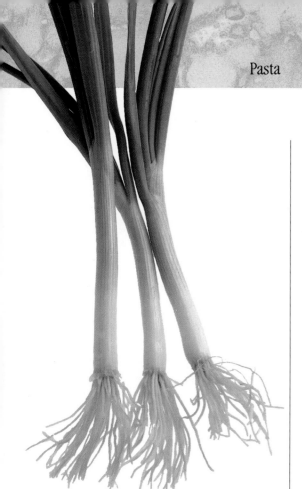

Shrimp Dumplings

These dumplings owe their refreshing lightness both to their ingredients and to the fact that they are steamed. They are best when served with a peppery hot dipping sauce.

500g (1 lb) shelled, deveined shrimps

2 tablespoons sesame oil

2 cloves garlic, chopped

1 teaspoon fresh ginger, chopped

6 water chestnuts, chopped

4 spring onions, chopped

2 tablespoons cornflour

salt and pepper to taste

60 won ton skins (ready-made, or see Chinese egg noodle recipe, page 41)

1. Cook the shrimps in the oil for about 5 minutes. Let them cool, then chop them as finely as you can.

2. Combine all of the ingredients except the won ton skins in a bowl.

3. Place a teaspoon of filling in the centre of each won ton wrapper. Fold the wrapper into a triangle and seal the edges.

4. Prepare your steamer by bringing the water to a boil. Oil the steamer rack if it is made of metal.

5. Place a single layer of dumplings into the steamer and cook for 10 minutes. Repeat until all of the dumplings are ready. Serves 4 to 6 as a meal, 8 to 12 as a first course.

Chicken Won Tons

You can boil or fry these won tons according to your taste, and serve them with a variety of dipping sauces such as the traditional soy sauce-rice vinegar combination, a hot mustard sauce or an orange duck sauce.

500g (1 lb) uncooked chicken meat

1 tablespoon sesame oil

1 large, dried shiitake mushroom

250g (8 oz) Chinese leaves

2 spring onions, chopped

1 teaspoon fresh ginger, chopped

1 clove garlic, chopped

1 tablespoon soy sauce

60 won ton skins (ready-made, or see Chinese egg noodle recipe, page 41)

vegetable oil for deep frying or chicken broth for boiling

1. Cook the chicken in the sesame oil until all of the meat loses its pink colour. Allow it to cool and then dice it finely.

2. Soak the mushroom in warm water, then chop it.

3. Clean, parboil, squeeze dry, and chop the Chinese leaves.

4. Combine all of the ingredients except the won ton skins and the vegetable oil or chicken broth. Process the mixture in a food processor or blender.

5. Place a teaspoon of filling in the centre of each won ton wrapper. Fold the wrapper into a triangle and seal the edges. Flip the ends of the folded edge in toward the centre of the triangle, and press the two points together.

6. To deep fry, heat the vegetable oil to about 180°C (350°F). Drop in the won tons and cook until golden brown.

7. To boil, heat the chicken broth to a rolling boil and drop in the won tons. When the water returns to a boil, reduce the heat and simmer the won tons for about 10 minutes. When they're done, the cooked won tons will float on the top of the broth.

8. Serve as a meal for 4 to 6, or as an hors d'oeuvre for about 12.

© Steven Mark Needham/Envision

© Felicia Martinez/PhotoEdit

Potato and Cheese Pierogi

Nothing is more warming than these Polish dumplings on a cold winter evening. Although they are usually served as the main course of the meal, they make a perfect side dish.

For The Filling:

5 medium potatoes

1 large onion, chopped

1/4 pound farmer or cottage cheese

2 tablespoons butter

salt and pepper to taste

For The Dough:

3 cups flour

1 cup sour cream

1 egg

1. Clean and peel the potatoes, cut them into quarters, and place them in a pot with just enough water to cover them. Cover the pot and boil the potatoes for 20 to 40 minutes, until tender. Drain them as soon as they are done.

2. While the potatoes are cooking, mix all of the ingredients for the dough together and knead until the dough has a consistent texture. Add flour if it is too sticky, or water if it is too dry. Cover and set the dough aside while you prepare the filling.

3. Mash the potatoes while they are still warm. Fry the onion in the butter. Combine the potatoes, onion, and cheese in a bowl and mix well, adding salt and pepper if desired.

4. Knead the dough a few times and roll it out onto a floured surface. When the sheet of dough is about 1/8 inch thick, cut it into 2- or 3-inch circles.

5. Drop about 1 tablespoon of filling onto the center of each round. Moisten the exposed dough with water and fold each circle in half. Seal the open edges of the semicircle by pressing them together.

6. Boil the pierogi for 5 to 8 minutes in salted water. Drain and serve them with melted butter and sour cream. This recipe will serve 4 as a main dish and 6 to 8 as a side dish.

Hearty Beef Dumplings

This is delicious served plain or with butter, gravy or tomato sauce.

1 pound pasta all'uovo (see page 26)

3/4 pound lean ground beef

1 medium onion, chopped

2 tablespoons olive oil

salt and pepper to taste

1 teaspoon fresh chopped marjoram

2 tablespoons fresh chopped parsley

1. Prepare the pasta dough and set it aside to rest.

2. Cook the beef and onion in the olive oil. Allow it to cool.

3. Combine all of the ingredients except the pasta in a bowl and mix well.

4. Roll out the dough into a sheet about 1/8 inch thick. Cut it into circles 2 or 3 inches in diameter.

5. Place a teaspoon of filling onto each round, and fold it over into a semicircle. Pinch the edges to seal them.

6. Boil the dumplings for 10 to 15 minutes. Serves 4 to 6.

© Felicia Martirez/PhotoEdit

COOKING THE PASTA

Can anybody cook pasta? Surprisingly, the answer is yes and no. Pasta is a simple dish, but amateur chefs frequently lack a complete understanding of how it should be handled. Most people can prepare acceptable noodle dishes but do not realize that, with a few refinements in technique, they could make perfect pasta.

With the exception of some Asian and Middle Eastern varieties, all noodles should be cooked according to the instructions listed below. Follow these steps to prepare pasta that's perfectly cooked and ready to sauce and eat.

1. 500g (1 lb) of uncooked pasta will yield enough to serve 4 to 6 as a main course and 6 to 8 as a first course. 4.8 litres (8 pints) of water will cook 500g (1 lb) of pasta. Do not attempt to cook more than 500g (1 lb) of pasta at a time. Otherwise your noodles will cook unevenly and stick together in clumps. Before you start cooking your pasta, place a colander in the sink to drain the finished noodles. Your sauce and guests should also be ready and waiting so that the pasta can be served at the peak of its flavour.

2. Put the water in a large pan. Add 1 tablespoon of salt for a full 500g (1 lb) of pasta, to bring out its flavour, and 1 tablespoon of olive oil, to keep the water from foaming over. Bring it to a hard boil.

3. Place the pasta in the boiling water a bit at a time so the water doesn't stop boiling, but be sure to add all the pasta within 1 minute or it will cook unevenly. With long pasta such as spaghetti, drop the strands into the water vertically and bend them into the water with a fork as they soften. Stir the pasta occasionally to ensure that each piece floats freely. If the water stops boiling while you add the noodles, cover the pan so that the water returns to a boil as quickly as possible.

4. Stir the pasta occasionally while it cooks. There's no way to tell exactly how long pasta will take to cook, but you can be reasonably certain that the cooking time given for packaged pasta is too long. Fresh noodles require 1 to 8 minutes in the pan, while dry pasta

generally cooks in 4 to 20 minutes, depending on its shape and age. Start testing your pasta for doneness after 1 minute for fresh, and 4 minutes for dry, and continue testing it at 30-second intervals by lifting noodles from the pan with a fork and biting them. Pasta is done when it has lost its floury taste all the way to its centre yet still offers some resistance to the bite. Pasta cooked in this way, to retain a slight firmness, is called *al dente* (literally, "to the tooth").

5. As soon as the pasta has finished cooking, pour the contents of the pan into a colander in your sink. Do not rinse the pasta unless the recipe calls for rinsing, or the pasta is for a salad or will be stored for later use. Shake the colander gently to remove excess water from the drained noodles, and pour these into a large, warm, buttered or oiled serving bowl. Toss the pasta with the oil, top it with sauce or grated cheese, and serve it immediately.

6. To save cooked pasta that is to be served later, rinse the hot, drained noodles thoroughly in cold water. Toss the pasta with some oil so that it will not stick together, and store it in an airtight container in the refrigerator. To reheat the noodles, plunge them into a pan of boiling water for 3 minutes, and stir them so they don't stick together. Drain and serve as outlined above.

The most notable exceptions to this noodle-cooking technique are couscous, which is prepared by steaming (see page 132 for recipe), and Asian rice sticks and bean threads (cellophane noodles), which need only a brief soaking before being added to the other ingredients in a recipe (see page 137). In addition, pasta destined for baking dishes, *pasta al forno,* requires only parboiling for about one-third the normal cooking time before it is cooked in a casserole. To parboil pasta, follow the instructions given above and simply reduce the cooking time.

3 Pasta Sauces

THE BEST SAUCES

While pasta can be beautiful, delicious and certainly nutritious on its own, where would it be without sauce? What you put on top of the pasta is at least as important to the success of a pasta dish as the pasta you use. Pasta usually has a rather mild flavour. Sauce harmonizes with this subtle taste, giving it more life and making it more complex. Sauce adds greatly to the nutrition of pasta dishes. And don't forget the importance of serving a beautiful meal. Sauce is integral to the visual impact your pasta makes when you place it in front of your guests.

Because the various pastas are so adaptable, you can choose from an incredible variety of sauces in several different forms—a melange of seasonal vegetables, a hearty meal ragoût a creamy blend of cheeses, a simple glaze of olive oil and fresh garlic or even a delicious traditional tomato sauce.

Not all pastas stand up well to sauce, however. Central European, Middle Eastern, and Asian noodles rarely appear topped with the fluid sauces that typically grace Italian-style pasta. Instead, these noodles most often show up in soups, smothered with stews, or unadorned. For that reason, this section limits itself to "sauce" in the traditional sense, and presents recipes designed primarily to top off Italian-style pastas.

But don't worry, you won't run out of ideas for serving pastas with sauces. The possible combinations are endless.

Marinara Sauce is easier and faster to prepare than Classic Tomato Sauce. But that doesn't mean it isn't delicious. This version has been enriched with artichoke hearts and mushrooms, to make a sauce that tastes special, but requires very little extra time.

Making Sauce

The 10 recipes given here represent popular basic pasta sauces that every cook should know how to prepare. You will find them very easy to make and store, and might want to cook up large batches for freezing. Once you discover how rich these sauces taste and how convenient they are you may give up store-bought sauces forever.

These sauces not only yield dazzling results in their original forms, they also provide great starting-points for improvisation. You can add fresh vegetables to the tomato sauce, vodka and tomato paste to the Bechamel, walnuts to the pesto—whatever your taste buds allow. Each recipe gives ideas for alterations, and the primavera recipe is just a set of guidelines that freely allows you to make best use of seasonal produce. If you use your imagination and experiment when making a sauce, you're bound to create something special.

Sauces can use many more ingredients than just tomatoes, garlic and oil. Lemon, butter, cream, basil, fresh black pepper and more can be combined to make a wonderful sauce for pasta. Let your taste buds lead you to create personal variations on the classic sauce recipes.

© Michael Grand

Classic Tomato Sauce

This most essential of sauces has an infinite number of renditions, and remains the most familiar and beloved pasta topping.

1 medium onion, chopped

2 cloves garlic, chopped

15g (1/2 oz) fresh basil, chopped

2 stalks celery, chopped

1 carrot, chopped

2 tablespoons olive oil

1kg (2 lb) fresh or two 440g (14 oz) cans plum tomatoes

salt and pepper to taste

1/2 teaspoon sugar (optional)

1. Sauté the onion, garlic, basil, celery and carrot in the olive oil until the onion is transparent.

2. If you are using fresh tomatoes, peel them by dipping them in boiling water for 30 seconds and slipping off the skin. Cut off the stem end and squeeze the seeds out of the tomato. If you are using canned tomatoes, drain them and reserve the liquid.

3. Chop the fresh or canned tomato flesh and mix it with the sautéed ingredients in a pan. Bring the mixture to a boil, then reduce the heat to a simmer.

4. Cook the sauce, uncovered over lowest heat, for 30 to 45 minutes, until it thickens. Stir it occasionally to ensure that it does not burn. Add a bit of the tomato juice if the sauce seems too thick.

5. Purée one half of the sauce in a blender or food processor and mix it with the rest of the sauce. If needed, add some of the reserved canning liquid or water. Season to taste with salt, pepper, and sugar. Yields about 1.2 liters (2 pints) of sauce.

Variations: Season with oregano, thyme, bay, or tarragon. Add 250g (8 oz) of sautéed, sliced mushrooms; 60g (2 oz) of pitted, sliced black olives; or 185g (6 oz) cooked, diced prawns. Leave out the celery and carrot, add 185ml (6 fl oz) of double cream and purée the entire batch of sauce.

Marinara Sauce

You can prepare this light, simple tomato sauce in about half the time it takes to make classic sauce.

5 cloves garlic, chopped

2 tablespoons olive oil

1kg (2 lb) fresh or two 440g (14 oz) cans plum tomatoes

1 teaspoon dried oregano

3 tablespoons fresh chopped parsley

salt and pepper to taste

1. Sauté the garlic in the olive oil for several seconds.

2. If you are using fresh tomatoes, peel them by dipping them in boiling water for 30 seconds and removing the skin. Cut off the stem end and squeeze the seeds out of the tomato. If you are using canned tomatoes, drain the liquid.

3. Chop the tomatoes and add them to the pan with the garlic, along with the oregano, parsley and salt and pepper. Bring the mixture to a boil, then reduce the heat and simmer for 15 to 20 minutes, uncovered. Makes about 1.2 litres (2 pints).

© Burke/Triolo

Bolognese Sauce

This rich meat sauce, a traditional Italian offering, derives its savoriness from a complex interplay of many-flavored ingredients. It is the perfect topping for spaghetti.

1 ounce dried mushrooms

3 tablespoons olive oil

1/4 cup minced prosciutto

1 carrot, diced

1 small onion, chopped

1/2 pound lean ground beef

1/2 cup dry red wine

3 tablespoons tomato paste

1 strip lemon peel

1 tablespoon chopped parsley

pinch of nutmeg

salt and pepper to taste

1. Soak the dried mushrooms in water for about 15 minutes, until softened.

2. Cook the prosciutto, carrot, and onion in the olive oil until the onion is transparent. Add the meat, mushrooms, and soaking liquor and stir over medium-high heat.

3. When the meat is thoroughly cooked, add the wine and simmer until the alcohol has evaporated.

4. Add the remaining ingredients and cook, uncovered, over very low heat for 45 minutes. Makes about 2 cups.

Variations: Substitute ham or bacon for the prosciutto. Add 1 or 2 garlic cloves, $^1/_2$ cup of raisins, or $^1/_4$ cup of capers.

When the sauce has finished cooking, add $^1/_4$ cup of heavy cream.

Bechamel Sauce

Baked dishes such as lasagna often include this white sauce, but bechamel also serves as a basic ingredient in many other sauce recipes.

2 tablespoons butter

2 tablespoons flour

2 cups milk

salt to taste

white pepper to taste

1. Melt the butter over low heat and use a whisk to mix in the flour. Cook, stirring constantly, for 2 or 3 minutes, to yield a smooth golden roux.

2. Add the cold milk quickly while you continue to stir. Slowly bring the sauce to a boil, then reduce the heat to a simmer and add salt, pepper, and nutmeg to taste.

3. Cook over lowest heat for 20 to 40 minutes until the sauce thickens. Makes approximately two cups.

Variations: For a richer sauce, substitute 1/4 cup of heavy cream for the same amount of milk.

Add 1/2 cup grated Parmesan cheese to make Mornay sauce.

Season with garlic and herbs and add a cup of cooked shellfish or fish for a creamy white seafood sauce.

© Burke/Triolo

Bechamel Sauce is the starting point for this wonderful dish of steamed mussels with saffron cream served over fresh fettucine. To the basic sauce you add a touch of saffron, garlic, a hint of red pepper and fresh, steamed mussels.

Basic Meat Sauce

Minced beef adds both flavour and texture to sauces, and goes particularly well with tomatoes. This version and its countless variations can top off just about any kind of pasta.

2 tablespoons olive oil

1 medium onion, chopped

2 cloves garlic, chopped

90g (3 oz) sliced mushrooms

1 green pepper, chopped

500g (1 lb) lean minced beef

1kg (2 lb) fresh or two 440g (14 oz) cans plum tomatoes

125ml (4 fl oz) dry red wine

1 tablespoon dried basil

1 bay leaf

salt and pepper to taste

1. Heat the olive oil and add the onion, garlic, mushrooms and green pepper. Cook over medium heat for about 20 minutes.

2. Raise the heat and add the meat to the vegetables. Stir constantly while cooking until the meat has lost all of its pinkness. Reduce the heat.

3. If you are using fresh tomatoes, peel them by dipping them in boiling water for 30 seconds and slipping off the skin. Cut off the stem end and squeeze the seeds out of the tomato. If you are using canned tomatoes, drain the liquid.

4. Chop the tomatoes and add them to the meat mixture. Add the wine and seasonings.

5. Cover the pan and simmer the sauce for 1½ hours, stirring occasionally, until it thickens slightly. Yields approximately 1.5 litres (2½ pints).

Variations: Add chopped celery or carrots, or diced spicy sausage or pancetta (Italian bacon).

Season with oregano or cloves.

Alfredo Sauce

Although most often associated with fettucine, this sauce complements any fresh pasta, including stuffed varieties such as tortellini.

60g (2 oz) unsalted butter

60ml (2 fl oz) double cream

60g (2 oz) grated Parmesan cheese

salt and pepper to taste

1. Prepare 500g (1 lb) of the noodles. Drain and place them hot in a warm serving bowl.

2. Cut up the butter into small chunks and add it with the cream, cheese and seasonings to the pasta.

3. Toss the contents of bowl to distribute the sauce evenly over the noodles. Serve immediately.

Variations: Add fresh cooked peas and strips of prosciutto, ham or bacon.

© Michael Grand

Simple Garlic and Oil

You can do nothing tastier to your homemade pasta than to toss it in this delicate blend of garlic and olive oil. The addition of steamed or canned clams or mussels easily transforms this recipe into one of the most satisfying sauces around.

1/2 cup olive oil

4 cloves garlic, minced

1. Sauté the garlic in the oil over low heat until it just starts to brown. Do not overcook the garlic, or the sauce will be bitter.

2. Toss the garlic and oil with a pound of piping hot pasta, and garnish with fresh chopped parsley and grated Parmesan cheese. Serve immediately.

Variations: Add a crushed red chili pepper while cooking, or oil-cured black olives to the garnish.

Add black pepper or oregano for extra seasoning. Steam 2 dozen clams or mussels in wine or water and add them to the oil, in or out of their shells. You may substitute a 10-ounce can of whole or minced clams for fresh ones.

Creamy Red Pepper Sauce

Light, sweet and creamy, this sauce has a pleasing hint of smokiness from the roasted peppers. It's ideal for the most delicate pastas.

4 sweet red peppers

2 tablespoons olive oil

2 cloves garlic, minced

2 tablespoons sherry

1 cup light cream

salt and pepper to taste

1. Roast the peppers under the broiler, turning them as each side chars and blisters. When they are thoroughly blackened, remove and allow them to cool in a paper bag that is folded shut. Take them out and slip the skins off. Cut the peppers open to remove their seeds. Dice the flesh.

2. Cook the garlic in the oil for several minutes, then add the red peppers, sherry and salt and pepper. Bring the contents of the pan to a boil, then reduce the heat and simmer for 10 minutes.

3. Place the pepper mixture in a blender or food processor and puree. Add the cream and process until the sauce is well mixed. Return the sauce to low heat until ready to serve. Yields about a pint.

Variations: Season with fresh basil or tarragon or substitute vodka for the sherry.

Garnish with black olives or capers.

Perfect Pesto

This basil paste complements a wide variety of pasta dishes, including cold pasta salads. Just remember never to heat pesto before putting it on pasta, or it will separate.

2 packed cups fresh basil leaves

4 cloves garlic, minced

1/4 cup pignoli (pine) nuts

1/2 cup grated Parmesan cheese

1/2 cup olive oil

salt and pepper to taste

1. Wash, pat dry, and stem the basil leaves.

2. Put the basil, garlic, pignoli nuts and salt in a mortar, blender or food processor. Pulverize until you have a smooth paste.

3. Add the cheese and mix until thoroughly combined. Blend in the olive oil. Salt and pepper to taste. Yields about 1$^1/_2$ cups.

Variations: Substitute pecorino Romano cheese for the Parmesan, or use a combination of the two. When basil is out of season, try parsley instead. Replace the pignoli nuts with walnuts.

© Michael Grand

Pasta Primavera

Primavera means "spring" in Italian, and indeed, young spring vegetables such as peas, asparagus, and green beans make an especially delightful complement to pasta. But you can use any season's fresh vegetables to create a colourful, tasty and healthful pasta topping.

Pasta primavera must contain only crisp, lightly cooked vegetables seasoned with fresh herbs and just enough salt and black pepper to bring out the dish's full flavor. Prepare about 185g (6 oz) of vegetable mixture for each main-course serving. That means you need a total of 750g (1½ lb) of cooked vegetables to serve 4 people; 1.1kg (2¼ lb) to serve 8. Measure each portion of vegetable after cutting it to the desired form. You can combine 3 or more ingredients in equal amounts or emphasize 1 or 2 of your best market selections, supplementing them with smaller amounts of other vegetables.

Sauté the vegetables in the barest minimum of olive oil, adding the longest-cooking ingredients first.

Cover the pan for a few minutes to steam the vegetables just before serving. Alternately, blanch or steam each component separately until just done, and toss the results together with seasonings. Serve the vegetables over fresh tagliatelle or fettucine if possible; otherwise, angel's hair or linguine make an acceptable base. To top it all off, grate on some Parmesan and grind on some black pepper, or drizzle a herbed Mornay sauce over the dish.

You can use just about any vegetable in past primavera, as long as it is fresh and cooks up nicely. The only rule to follow when choosing vegetable combinations is that you should strive for a variety of colours, textures, flavours and shapes. Here are the peak seasons for various vegetables, and a suggested combination for each season.

Year-round vegetables: carrots, celery, garlic, most herbs, cultivated mushrooms, onions, mange tout

Year-round combination: garlic, mushrooms

Spring vegetables: artichokes, asparagus, avocados, basil, broccoli, cauliflower, green beans, leeks, okra, peas, peppers, shallots, spinach, summer squash (yellow and courgettes)

Spring combination: asparagus, peas, red pepper, yellow squash

Summer vegetables: basil, beans, sweetcorn, okra, peppers, summer squash (yellow and courgettes), tomatoes

Summer combination: sweetcorn, okra, courgettes, tomatoes

Autumn vegetables: broccoli, cauliflower, leeks, okra, peppers, shallots, spinach, wild mushrooms

Autumn combination: broccoli, cauliflower, wild mushrooms

Winter vegetables: avocados, broccoli, cauliflower, leeks, shallots, spinach, wild mushrooms

Winter combination: shallots, spinach

© Carl Simowitz

PAIRING PASTA WITH SAUCE

Although some pasta snobs disagree, there are no hard-and-fast rules for matching pasta with sauce. Common sense should serve as your guide when you choose combinations, but here are some tips:

1. Fresh and stuffed pastas do not generally require as much extra seasoning as dry pasta. The delicate flavor of fresh pasta is overwhelmed by robust sauces, so choose light toppings such as garlic and oil, butter and cheese, seafood, fresh vegetables and herbs. When saucing filled pasta, make sure your topping complements the pasta stuffing.

2. Dry pasta stands up well to assertive sauces. Curved and tubular shapes catch lots of sauce, so use them with chunky, stew-like toppings. This combination gives you a generous portion of sauce on each forkful of pasta.

3. Very spicy or rich creamy sauces should top flat or cylindrical strands that won't pick up too much liquid. Use more subtle seasonings on thin strands.

4. Three types of pasta shapes adapt well to baked pasta dishes: short, tubular shapes; large, rectangular shapes; and large, fillable shapes. Macaroni, ziti, penne and similar forms remain evenly distributed throughout the sauce while baking. Lasagna makes perfect layers between fillings and sauces. Cannelloni and large shells are designed for filling and baking, and stay in place in the pan.

5. Pastas made from durum semolina do best in pasta salads, because they retain their integrity even when exposed to dressings for long periods of time. Fresh pasta and soft wheat noodles, on the other hand, absorb too much liquid and grow soggy too quickly for use in pasta salads.

© Burke/Triolo

This piquant tomato sauce is a good mate for the large shells underneath it. The flavorful bits and chunks in this sauce will be trapped in the ridges and openings of the shells, so each bite will hold delicious rewards.

4 Pasta Parties

ENTERTAINING WITH PASTA

There are several useful things to know about having a memorable pasta party, whether it is an intimate dinner for 2 or a bash for 25; an elegant sit-down soiree or a merry children's birthday.

Be advised that the key to any successful pasta party is planning. Once you decide to have a party, think about the type of event you want to host, and how you can best put it together. Several considerations should guide you:

• Consider the party's purpose. Will it celebrate a birthday, anniversary, graduation, wedding, or a retirement? Or do you just feel like getting together with friends? Each of these events calls for a different approach.

• Think of your guests. How many would you like to invite? Who will they be, and what are their tastes? Obviously, your family requires different treatment than your professional colleagues.

• Examine your budget. How much can you afford to spend? It's safe to assume that the party will cost more than you expect.

• Evaluate you and your kitchen's capabilities and limitations. Are you a novice cook? How much time do you have to get ready? Can your kitchen handle food preparation for 20 guests? Do you own the necessary equipment to prepare and serve enough food? Is your refrigerator large enough to store everything?

Keeping all these factors in mind, you can choose from a wide array of party possibilities: indoor or outdoor; formal or informal; breakfast, brunch, luncheon, cocktails, or early or late dinner; buffet or sit-down. Decide if you can juggle all of the details on your own, or if you will need help. Will you need to rent furniture, glassware or other supplies? Analyze your home as a space for entertaining, and figure out how to set it up so your guests will be most comfortable. Carefully plan the decor, lighting and background music. Know ahead of time what will and will not work.

Although every host feels tempted to dazzle guests with elaborate, extravagant galas, most people have more success with relatively practical, straightforward parties. Imposing decorations and table settings will usually make guests feel uncomfortable rather than festive. Menus fit for the gods too often fail in the hands of merely mortal chefs. And exotic food can frighten timid diners. Both you and your guests will enjoy the event if you relax, keep it simple, be yourself—and let the food speak for itself.

Keeping it simple, however, does not mean that you have to stick to spaghetti and meatballs. Your party, after all, should be something special, and the food you serve should be extraordinary. As the suggested menus that accompany the following recipes demonstrate, you can serve truly unforgettable repasts without spending endless days in the kitchen. Many of the dishes—or parts of them—can be prepared ahead of time and reheated or served cold or at room temperature. You finish as much party work as possible before the guests arrive. Buffet-style service—a boon to any harried host—suits many of these menus, because almost every pasta dish stands up well to repeated scooping and stirring, and few require cutting at the serving table or on the plate. And the recipes can serve more guests than expected: All you have to do is boil up another pot of noodles and heat a little extra sauce.

Designed to delight and amuse even the pickiest guests, the party ideas outlined here work best if you apply a healthy dose of imagination. Each idea suggests a mood and a menu centered around pasta, and gives the recipe for the noodle dish. Choose the party that's best for you, plan carefully, and prepare for the festivities well in advance. But most of all, have a good time. If you do, your guests are bound to follow suit.

You can have a party that's as light and refreshing as a summer romance by serving Herb Ravioli with Walnut Sauce as your centrepiece. Start the meal with smoked trout and horseradish sauce, and follow the ravioli with a salad of Belgian endive and watercress with raspberry vinaigrette.

All these dishes (except the ravioli) taste best when served just slightly cool. You can prepare everything ahead of time, saving only the cooking of the ravioli for the last minute. Set the mood with a simple yet elegant floral arrangement and your best silver, crystal and china laid out on white linen. Wait for the sun to go down, then light a single white taper-candle and see what else ignites.

Chilled brut champagne or Frascati, a crisp, dry Italian white, would complement this meal perfectly.

Herb Ravioli

For the dough:

185g (6 oz) plain flour • 2 eggs • 1/2 teaspoon salt (optional)
1½ teaspoons olive oil (optional) • salt to taste

For the filling:

45g (1½ oz) fresh basil leaves • 2 cloves garlic • 2 tablespoons pine nuts
30g (1 oz) grated Parmesan cheese • 60ml (2 fl oz) olive oil

Prepare the pasta all'uovo (about 250g [8 oz]) according to the instructions on page 26.

Prepare the pesto filling (185ml [6 fl oz]) according to the instructions on page 93.

Fill the ravioli with pesto according to the procedure described on page 56.

When ready to serve, boil the ravioli for about 7 minutes. Drain and place them in two shallow bowls. Top with the walnut sauce and serve.

Serves 2

Walnut Sauce

125g (4 oz) shelled walnuts • 2 tablespoons breadcrumbs • 1 clove garlic
2 tablespoons olive oil • 75ml (2½ fl oz) milk • salt to taste

Blanch the walnuts in boiling water and rub off their skins. Soak the breadcrumbs in water, then drain and squeeze them dry.

Place the walnuts, breadcrumbs, and garlic in a mortar, blender, or food processor and blend until a smooth paste forms.

Add the olive oil, milk, and salt to taste and stir well.

Serves 2

*P*asta for breakfast? Why not? And why not make someone's morning memorable with a decadent breakfast in bed? Get up a little early, sneak into the kitchen, and whip up an easy yet delightful meal for two that includes fresh brioche, salad of pink grapefruit, oranges and red grapes and Spaghetti alla Carbonara. Spread a cloth napkin on a breakfast tray, tuck a single rose among the dishes and present the meal with the morning paper.

To make things a little easier, bake the brioche and mix up the fruit cocktail a day ahead, and pre-dice the meat and store it covered in the refrigerator. Put the coffee on to brew and the brioche in to warm before you start cooking the spaghetti. If you like, serve the breakfast with a glass of champagne, a mimosa, or a bloody mary.

Spaghetti alla Carbonara

3 ounces pancetta or bacon • 1 tablespoon olive oil • 8 ounces dry spaghetti • 2 eggs
2 tablespoons light cream • 1/3 cup grated Parmesan cheese • salt and pepper to taste

Dice the pancetta or bacon into small pieces. Heat the olive oil, then add the meat. Cook it until the fat is transparent, then set it aside.

Put the spaghetti on to boil. Beat the eggs in a bowl, then mix in the cream, Parmesan cheese, salt, and pepper.

When the spaghetti is *al dente,* drain it and place it in a large bowl. Immediately begin pouring the egg mixture over the hot pasta, tossing rapidly so that the eggs do not set in chunks. After adding the eggs, toss in the pancetta or bacon and serve.

Serves 2

*T*wo Sides Brown, thought by some to be the ancestor of American chow mein, is an ideal party dish. These crunchy-on-the-outside, tender-on-the-inside fried noodle patties are both unusual and visually stimulating. You can top them with all kinds of Chinese mixtures, from curried shrimp to pork Peking style, so you'll never run out of ways to serve this exciting dish. Try serving them with egg drop soup, egg rolls and black mushrooms with bamboo shoots.

To set an authentic mood, dust off your chopsticks and get out your Chinese soup bowls and ceramic soup spoons. Accent the table with red, the Chinese color of celebration, perhaps with red napkins or an arrangement of red carnations. Brew some tea or serve the meal with Chinese beer, or pour some Gewurztraminer, a flavorful white wine.

Two Sides Brown with Beef and Ginger

1/2 pound Chinese egg noodles · *2 tablespoons sesame oil*
1 tablespoon fresh ginger, minced · *2 cloves garlic, minced*
1/2 pound lean beef, in strips · *2 scallions, chopped* · *2 stalks celery, chopped*
1/2 pound green beans · *3/4 cup beef bouillon* · *2 tablespoons soy sauce*
2 tablespoons sherry · *1/8 teaspoon hot oil* · *1 tablespoon corn starch*
1/3 cup peanut oil

Cook the noodles in boiling water until they are just barely done—2 or 3 minutes. Drain and rinse them, then toss them in a bowl with about a teaspoon of the sesame oil.

Heat the remainder of the sesame oil in a wok. Add the ginger and garlic and stir fry for 30 seconds. Mix in the beef and stir fry until it begins to change color.

Add the scallions, celery and green beans to the wok and continue to stir fry for 2 minutes. Stir in the beef bouillon, soy sauce, sherry, hot oil and corn starch. Mix thoroughly, reduce the heat and cover.

Pour half of the peanut oil into a 12-inch cast-iron frying pan. Heat the pan until the oil almost smokes, then put all the noodles in the pan. Press the noodles into a pancake and cook for about 5 minutes, until the bottom browns.

Remove the noodle cake to a plate, add the rest of the peanut oil to the pan, and heat. Return the noodles to the pan, unbrowned side down, and cook until the second side browns.

Place the noodle cake on a serving plate, top it with the beef mixture and serve.

Serves 2

*G*oing on a picnic doesn't mean leaving the pasta at home. When the first warm days of spring beckon, call some friends and pack a wonderful picnic in a big wicker basket. Start with whole-wheat baguettes, vegetable pâté and assorted cheeses. Then serve this Chicken and Asparagus Pasta Salad, followed by fresh fruit and nuts.

Gather together a bright buffalo plaid or trapper's blanket, some colorful plastic flatware and paper plates and find a nice, sunny spot for an afternoon picnic. Of course, this menu can work just as well in the comfort of your own home, either as brunch, lunch or a light midnight repast. It requires little preparation, and is especially suited to last-minute entertaining. To bring out the best in this meal at any time of day, serve it with a light, fruity white wine such as a German Moselle or Rhone or a French Reisling.

Chicken and Asparagus Pasta Salad

For the salad:

12 ounces dry rotelle or fusilli · 1 whole chicken breast · 1 pound asparagus
6 water chestnuts, sliced · 1/2 cup coarsely chopped walnuts

For the dressing:

2/3 cup olive oil · 1/3 cup lemon juice · 2 cloves garlic, pressed
1 teaspoon dried tarragon · salt and white pepper to taste

Cook the pasta *al dente,* then drain and rinse it. Toss it with a little olive oil and set it aside.

Bake the chicken breast at 350 degrees for about 45 minutes, until done. Allow the breast to cool, remove the skin, bone it and slice the meat into 1-inch strips.

Steam the asparagus until tender. When it is cool, cut it into 1-inch pieces.

Combine the pasta, chicken, asparagus, water chestnuts and walnuts in a large bowl.

Mix all of the dressing ingredients together. Pour half of the dressing over the salad and toss well. Add more dressing if desired, then refrigerate the salad until you are ready to serve it.

Serves 4

*D*inner parties limited to 4 have a quiet intimacy that makes them both relaxed and sophisticated. Here's a menu that is perfect for a small party in early spring, when the season's first tender shoots of asparagus appear in the markets: vichyssoise to start, followed by Lobster Agnolotti, asparagus with hollandaise sauce and a dessert of baba au rhum.

Use your finest tableware, candlesticks and decorations to create an ambience of understated luxury to match this gourmet menu. Soft lighting and music will enhance the evening's aura of almost decadent pleasure. Full-bodied French or California white wines, such as Chardonnay and Sauvignon Blanc, go well with this meal.

Lobster Agnolotti

For the dough:
3 cups flour • 4 eggs • 1 teaspoon salt (optional)
1 tablespoon olive oil (optional)

For the topping:
6 tablespoons butter • 3 tablespoons grated Parmesan cheese

For the filling:
Two 1 1/2 pound lobsters • 2 tablespoons butter
1/2 cup chopped shallots • 2 cloves garlic, minced • 1/2 teaspoon dried sage
1/2 teaspoon dried rosemary • 1/2 teaspoon dried thyme
2 ripe, fresh tomatoes, or 1 cup canned tomatoes, drained
2 tablespoons Cognac • 1/4 cup light cream • salt and pepper to taste

Boil the lobsters for about ten minutes in salted water. When they are cool enough to handle, remove the meat from the claws and tails. Dice the meat into small cubes.

Melt the butter and add the shallots, garlic and herbs. Sauté for 2 minutes.

If you are using fresh tomatoes, peel them by plunging them into boiling water for 30 seconds and then slipping their skins off. Cut off the stem end and squeeze out the seeds.

Chop the tomato flesh and add it to the sautéed herbs. Cook for 2 more minutes.

Add the lobster meat to the pan with the Cognac and cream. Season to taste and cook for 5 minutes.

Puree half of the lobster mixture in a blender or food processor. Mix the puree with the rest of the filling and allow it to cool.

Make the pasta dough according to the instructions on page 26.

Fill the agnolotti according to the instructions on page 56.

Cook the agnolotti in boiling water for about 8 minutes. Toss them in a large bowl with the melted butter, sprinkle on the grated Parmesan cheese, and serve immediately.

Serves 4

For a fresh and simple meal that combines some of summer's finest seasonal produce with ingredients available year-round, serve Spanish gazpacho, a seafood salad, Marian's Spaghetti and peach melba for dessert. This menu is well suited for those hot, sticky evenings when no one feels like cooking. And since the only warm dish on the menu—the spaghetti—requires only a few minutes at the stove, it's bound to become one of your favorite party menus.

Prepare everything but the spaghetti in advance to make mealtime more relaxed. Set the table with rustic Italian appointments, and create a centerpiece of summer wildflowers. To take advantage of soothing evening breezes, serve the meal al fresco. And to complement the food, serve a crisp, well-chilled white wine such as a Pinot Gris or Chenin Blanc.

Marian's Spaghetti

*6 large vine-ripened tomatoes · 1 pound dry spaghetti or linguine
1 cup heavy cream · 4 tablespoons olive oil
1 cup basil leaves, coarsely chopped and tightly packed · grated Parmesan cheese*

Peel the tomatoes by dipping them in boiling water for 30 seconds and slipping off their skins. Cut off their stem ends and squeeze out their seeds. Chop the flesh coarsely.

Put the spaghetti on to boil while you prepare the sauce.

Heat the cream and oil in a saucepan. When almost boiling, add the tomatoes.

Heat only until the tomatoes are hot—do not cook them. Remove the sauce from the heat and stir in the basil.

Drain the *al dente* spaghetti and toss it in a large bowl with the sauce. Serve immediately with grated Parmesan cheese on the side.

Serves 4

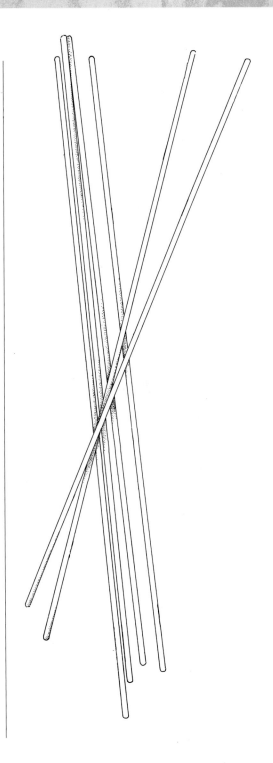

*F*all is the time to renew ties with old friends, and brunch offers an informal setting perfect for recounting tales of summertime adventure. A delightful menu might include buttermilk corn bread, Pumpkin Tortellini with Curry Sauce, spinach and goat cheese salad and spiced pears. Colorful, casual tableware heightens the mood, while a centerpiece of gourds, bittersweet, and turned leaves adds a seasonal touch.

The pumpkin tortellini included in this menu is made with amaretti, the crispy Italian macaroons usually sold in brightly colored tins. Topped with a slightly spicy, lightly sweet curry sauce, these tortellini make a wonderful brunch dish.

Be sure to have plenty of fresh-brewed coffee and tea on hand, as well as fruit juices. If your brunch is in the afternoon, serve a young, fruity red wine such as Beaujolais Nouveau or Lambrusco, a sparkling Italian number.

Pumpkin Tortellini

For the dough:

3 cups flour · 4 eggs · 1 teaspoon salt (optional) · 1 tablespoon olive oil (optional)

For the filling:

1 pumpkin, 1¹/₂–2 pounds · 8 amaretti
6 tablespoons grated Parmesan · nutmeg · salt and pepper to taste

Cut the pumpkin in half and scoop out the seeds. Slice the halves into wedges, peel off the skin, and place the pumpkin on a lightly greased baking pan. Bake for 20 minutes at 400 degrees.

Mash the cooked pumpkin through a sieve. If you prefer, you may substitute a 15-ounce can of unseasoned pumpkin pulp for the mashed fresh pumpkin.

Crush the amaretti in a mortar or with the side of a knife. Mix the crumbs, Parmesan, nutmeg, salt and pepper with the pumpkin.

Prepare the pasta all'uovo according to the instructions on page 26.

Fill the tortellini according to the instructions on page 60.

Cook the tortellini in boiling water for 10 minutes. Serve, topped with the curry sauce, in a large bowl.

Serves 6

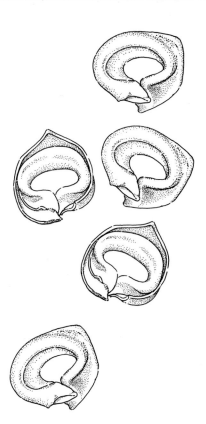

Curry Sauce

2 tart apples · medium onion, minced · 2 tablespoons olive oil
2 tablespoons curry powder · 1 cup light cream · 1 cup coconut milk
salt and pepper to taste

Peel, core and dice the apples.

Cook the apples and onion in the olive oil for 3 minutes.

Add the curry powder, mix well, then add the cream, coconut milk, salt and pepper. Cook for another minute.

Puree the sauce in a blender or food processor. Return the sauce to the pan and reheat it before pouring it over the pasta.

Serves 6

*I*n Thailand, the sweet-and-sour rice vermicelli dish known as mee krob is traditionally served on festive occasions. Why not spice up your next dinner party with an exotic menu built around this exquisite recipe for Mee Krob? It goes well with chicken and coconut milk soup, stir fried bok choi, steamed rice and papaya salad.

Mee Krob is perfect for friendly get-togethers where guests gravitate toward the kitchen, because it requires dramatic last-minute preparation. The noodles puff up instantaneously and sizzle temptingly when dropped into hot oil just before serving. Kick the dinner off with a snap, crackle and pop by inviting your guests to help you deep-fry the vermicelli.

Mee krob should be served the moment it's ready, so make sure everything else is in order before preparing it. Serve Thai beer if you can find it. Otherwise any pilsner will do.

Mee Krob

3 tablespoons fish sauce (available at Asian specialty stores, or use a mixture of 1 tablespoon each anchovy paste, soy sauce and water)

2 tablespoons lime juice • 1/4 cup white wine vinegar • 3 tablespoons soy sauce
4 tablespoons sugar • vegetable oil for frying • 3 cloves garlic, minced
1 medium onion, chopped • 2 dried chili peppers • 1/2 pound pork
1 pound small shelled and deveined shrimp • 1 whole chicken breast
6 dried Chinese mushrooms • 2 cups bean sprouts • 4 eggs • vegetable oil for frying
1/2 pound rice vermicelli • 6 tablespoons chopped coriander

Combine the fish sauce, lime juice, vinegar, soy sauce and sugar in a bowl and set aside.

Heat 2 tablespoons of oil in a wok and add the garlic and onion. Crumble the chili peppers into the wok and stir fry for 2 minutes.

Cut the pork into small strips and add it to the wok with the shrimp. Bone the chicken, cut it into strips, and stir it into the other ingredients. Cook the meat until just opaque.

Add the mushrooms (reconstituted in warm water for 15 minutes) and the bean sprouts. Cook until the shrimp are pink.

Scramble the eggs in a separate pan and cook until they are fairly dry. Mix the eggs into the meat with the sauce prepared at the beginning of the recipe. Stir thoroughly for a couple of minutes, then remove the mixture to a large bowl and cover.

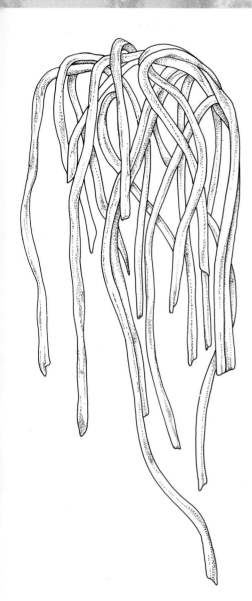

Wipe out the wok and use it to heat enough oil for deep frying (about 4 cups). Test the oil for readiness by dropping in small pieces of vermicelli. When a noodle puffs instantly in the oil, the oil is hot enough.

Drop the noodles, a handful at a time, into the oil. Turn them over when they stop sizzling and cook the second side until it no longer crackles. Use a slotted spoon to remove the vermicelli from the wok. Place the noodles on a paper towel to drain.

When all of the noodles are cooked, toss them gently with the meat mixture and serve topped with the chopped coriander.

Serves 6

Smoked salmon does as much for pasta as it does for bagels and cream cheese. That's why it works as well for brunch and lunch as it does for dinner. Surround it with cream of broccoli soup, a marinated mushroom salad and chocolate souffle.

Offering plenty of make-ahead options, this meal has the added advantage of using store-bought pasta secca. The sauce for the pasta takes only a few minutes to prepare, leaving you plenty of energy for the dessert souffle. Enjoy the dinner with a flavorful wine such as a Reisling, a good white or red Rioja, or a Pinot Noir.

Farfalle with Smoked Salmon

*1 pound dry farfalle · 1/2 pound smoked salmon · 1/2 cup butter
1 cup light cream · 5 egg yolks · salt and pepper to taste*

Cook the pasta while you start the sauce. Cut the salmon into small pieces.

Melt the butter in a pan over low heat. Put the salmon in the pan with the melted butter.

Drain the farfalle and add it to the pan.

Beat the egg yolks with the cream and pour the mixture over the pasta. Cook at low heat for a couple of minutes, stirring constantly so that the eggs do not set.

Pour the pasta into a large bowl and serve.

Serves 6

*G*nocchi, *those little Italian dumplings, make a perfect centerpiece for any party meal. They have a tantalizing and wonderful texture and can be fancy or plain depending on the mood of the party. To present Potato Gnocchi with Four Cheeses in an elegant setting, serve it with carpaccio of sirloin, sautéed spinach and cassis sorbet. Or just make a big bowl of the dumplings the focus of a family-style meal.*

To reduce party-time pressure, form the dumplings a day in advance, then simply boil them when you are ready to make the sauce. You can also prepare the sorbet the day before the party, and the carpaccio a few hours ahead of time, while the spinach will require only a few minutes of preparation before serving. Select a wine that goes well with cheese, the dominant flavor of the meal. Italian whites such as Verdicchio, Orvieto, and Trebbiano are particularly good choices to accompany this dinner.

Potato Gnocchi with Four Cheeses

For the gnocchi:

2 pounds potatoes · 2 cups flour · 2 beaten eggs

For the sauce:

1 cup heavy cream · 4 tablespoons butter · 4 ounces Gorgonzola, cubed
4 ounces Fontina, cubed · 4 ounces Gruyère, cubed
4 ounces grated Parmesan cheese · salt and pepper to taste

Peel the potatoes and boil them until tender. Drain well and mash them with a fork.

Add the flour and eggs to the potatoes and mix them together into a smooth dough. Knead the dough for a couple of minutes on a floured work surface.

Roll handfuls of the dough into sausage shapes about 3/4 inch in diameter. Cut the sausages into 1-inch segments. Use a butter knife to make an indentation diagonally across each lump of dough. Fold the dough in toward the hollow, then roll each dumpling under a fork to form ridges in the dough.

Boil the gnocchi for 5 or 10 minutes, until they rise to the surface of the water. Prepare the sauce while the gnocchi cook.

Heat the cream and butter in a saucepan until it is about to boil. Gradually add the cheeses, stirring constantly over medium-low heat. When the sauce is thick and just short of bubbling, remove it from the heat.

When the gnocchi are done cooking, drain them and pour them into the saucepan with the cheese. Toss them thoroughly and serve.

Serves 6

Guaranteed to lift spirits on a bitter winter night, a hearty Slavic meal is ideal for entertaining good friends who are ravenous after a day of skiing, skating or tobogganing. Start by serving smoked salmon on pumpernickel rounds with capers and olive oil, followed by hot borscht with sour cream, Beef and Sauerkraut Pierogi with Mushroom Gravy, beets and, for dessert, fruit compote.

You can prepare the entire menu ahead of time and simply reheat the borscht, pierogi and cabbage while enjoying the appetizer with your guests. Go ahead and use your everyday tableware for this casual meal—just make sure to light a cheery fire in the fireplace. You will find that wine really doesn't stand up to this meal. Ice-cold vodka is the authentic drink of choice, but if you would rather avoid the hard stuff, serve beer instead, preferably a porter or pale ale.

Beef and Sauerkraut Pierogi

For the dough:

4 1/2 cups flour • 1 1/2 cups sour cream • 1 egg

For the filling:

1 small onion, minced • 1 tablespoon butter • 2 pounds lean ground beef
2 cups sauerkrat, drained • salt and pepper to taste

Mix all of the ingredients for the dough together and knead until the dough has a consistent texture. If it is too sticky add some extra flour; if it is too dry, add a little water. Cover and set the dough aside while you prepare the filling.

Cook the onion in the butter until it is transparent. Add the beef and continue cooking, stirring to break up any lumps that may form. When the meat has lost its pinkness, remove it from the heat and drain off the grease.

Mix the sauerkraut with the beef. Process the mixture in a blender, food mill, or food processor. Add some sauerkraut juice if the paste is too dry.

Knead the dough a few times and roll it out on a floured surface. When the sheet of dough is about 1/8 inch thick, cut it into 2- or 3-inch circles.

Drop about 1 tablespoon of filling onto the center of each round. Moisten the exposed dough with water and fold each circle in half. Seal the open edges of the semi-circle by pressing them together.

Boil the pierogi for 5 to 8 minutes in salted water. Drain and serve them topped with the mushroom gravy.

Serves 8

Mushroom Gravy

8 tablespoons butter • 3/4 pound fresh mushrooms, sliced
1 small onion, minced • 6 tablespoons flour • 3 cups beef boullion
1 tablespoon marjoram • salt and pepper to taste

Sauté the mushrooms and onion in the butter until the onion is transparent.

Sprinkle in the flour and mix until the butter and flour form a smooth paste.

Add the boullion and seasonings. Stir constantly until the mixture reaches the boiling point and thickens. Serve over the pierogi.

Serves 8

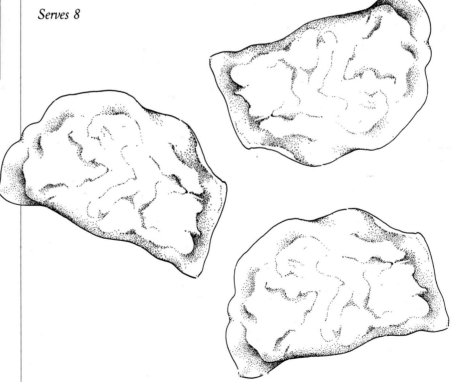

*T*una has something of a poor reputation because many people have only tasted it precooked and canned in heavy oil or salty water. But now that a wide variety of fresh fish are readily available, fresh tuna is easy to find. Not only is this firm, mild fish delicious, it is also rich in omega-3, a type of fat that is said by some people to have a positive effect on cardiovascular health. When combined with olives and capers in this recipe, fresh tuna adds a sophisticated touch to pasta. Start the meal with prosciutto with melon, follow that with Penne with Tuna, sauteed zucchini and tomatoes and a chocolate-walnut mousse cake. A Merlot or other dry red wine makes a nice complement to a menu centered around fresh tuna.

Penne with Tuna

2 pounds fresh tuna · 2 dozen calamata olives · 4 cloves garlic, minced
2 tablespoons olive oil · 1/3 cup capers · 28-ounce can crushed tomatoes
salt and pepper to taste · 1 pound dry penne

Cut the tuna into bite-sized pieces. Pit the olives and cut them into quarters.

Sauté the garlic for 1 or 2 minutes in the olive oil, then add the tuna, olives and capers. Cook until the tuna changes color.

Add the crushed tomatoes to the pan, season with salt and pepper and continue cooking at low to medium heat.

Cook and drain the penne. Put it in a large bowl and top with the sauce. Serve with grated Parmesan cheese.

Serves 8

*T*o inspire an air of continental conviviality among your guests, serve this menu: baguettes with sweet creamery butter, basil-tomato soup, Goat Cheese Tortelleti, salad of arugula and sorrel with poppyseed dressing and a hazelnut torte.

Strike the mood of the Gallic countryside by setting the table with great baskets of bread, a wooden salad bowl and a stoneware soup tureen and pasta bowl. Or, if you prefer, give the meal an upper-crust flair by hiring staff to serve the meal course by course.

This menu adapts well to brunches as well as dinner parties, and on hot days you can serve the soup cold. The recipe below calls for a pasta topping of butter and Parmesan cheese, but in cooler weather you might want to top the tortelleti with tomato sauce and use a different soup in the menu. An assertive white Burgundy or a light French red—such as Beaujolais or young red Bordeaux—goes perfectly with the goat cheese that is the heart of the meal.

Goat Cheese Tortelleti

For the dough:

4¹/₂ cups flour • 6 eggs • 1¹/₂ teaspoon salt (optional)
5 teaspoons olive oil (optional)

For the filling:

3 cups chopped goat cheese • 1¹/₂ cups ricotta cheese
1/4 cup heavy cream • 5 teaspoons fresh chopped chives • 2 eggs

For the topping:

1 cup butter • 1/2 cup grated Parmesan cheese

Prepare the dough according to the instructions on pages 26.

Mix all of the ingredients for the filling together in a bowl until smooth and well blended.

Prepare the tortelleti using the procedure described on pages 62.

Cook the tortelleti in boiling water for about 5 minutes. Toss with the butter and Parmesan and serve.

Serves 8

F ire up the grill, string up some lights and invite your friends over for a late-summer cookout. Serve a menu of French bread, steamed clams with melted butter, Rotelle Salad with Marinated Vegetables, shish kebabs of beef, peppers, onions and tomatoes, corn on the cob and blueberry pie. Set up your party as a do-it-yourself affair with baskets of bread and a great bowl of pasta salad from which diners can dish out their own portions. A chafing dish on the buffet table will keep the steamers warm, and platters of pre-cut vegetables and meat will tempt your guests to construct their own kebabs. Grill the corn alongside the kebabs, and let guests strip the husks themselves.

This no-fuss menu demands paper plates and plastic flatware, making cleanup quick and easy. Offer guests a chilled, dry, white wine such as a Chablis or Soave, and an ice cold lager beer such as a pilsner.

Rotelle Salad with Marinated Vegetables

For the salad:

1 large red pepper, chopped · 1/4 pound whole small mushrooms
1/4 pound steamed green beans · 1/4 pound steamed wax beans
1 medium zucchini, cubed · 2 carrots, sliced · 1 pound dried rotelle

For the marinade:

1 cup olive oil · 1/2 cup white wine vinegar
2 teaspoons prepared mustard · 2 teaspoons dried tarragon
2 teaspoons dried basil · 2 teaspoons dried thyme
salt and pepper to taste

Prepare the vegetables and put them in a large bowl. Combine all the ingredients for the marinade in a large jar and shake well.

Toss the marinade and the vegetables together. Cover the bowl with plastic wrap and refrigerate for 24 hours, stirring occasionally.

Four hours before serving the pasta salad, cook the rotelle. Drain and rinse it, then combine it with the vegetables and marinade.

Refrigerate the salad until half an hour before serving time, tossing it periodically. Allow it to warm slightly before serving.

Serves 8

A delightful meal at any time of year might include toasted garlic and herb bread, mushroom-stuffed artichokes, Pork and Spinach Cannelloni with Tomato Sauce, a mixed green salad with anise dressing and chocolate meringue.

You can prepare the artichokes and cannelloni for baking in advance and pop them into the oven just before your dinner. The only dish that must wait until the last minute is the calamari, which should be eaten immediately after it is fried.

Use your best table settings to make the meal elegant, or serve it as an informal dinner. Serve an unpretentious Italian Bardolino or Chianti throughout the meal.

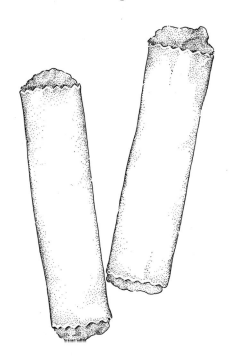

Pork and Spinach Cannelloni

For the dough:

6 cups flour • 8 eggs • 2 teaspoons salt (optional)
2 tablespoons olive oil (optional)

For the filling:

2 pounds fresh spinach • 4 tablespoons butter • 1 large onion, chopped
2 carrots, chopped • 2 celery sticks, chopped • 1 cup fresh parsley, chopped
3 pounds lean ground pork • 3/4 cup sherry • one 6-ounce can tomato paste
3/4 cup grated Parmesan cheese • 3 eggs • salt, pepper and nutmeg to taste

Prepare the pasta all'uovo according to the instructions on page 26.

Clean, parboil, pat dry and coarsely chop the spinach. Sauté it in the melted butter for a minute or so.

Add the onion, carrots, celery, and parsley and cook until the onion is transparent.

Mix in the pork and stir while continuing to cook. When the meat has lost its pinkness, add the sherry. Simmer until the alcohol has evaporated.

Stir in the tomato paste, cover the pan, and cook at lowest heat for about an hour. Stir periodically and add water if the mixture becomes too dry.

Beat the eggs and add them to the meat mixture along with the Parmesan cheese. Allow the filling to cool.

Prepare and fill the cannelloni according to the instructions on page 58. Place them in a large baking pan, top with tomato sauce and sprinkle with Parmesan. Bake at 450 degrees for 15 to 20 minutes and serve.

Serves 12

What better dish to serve to a gathering of your child's friends than Macaroni and Cheese, gooey and rich inside, and crispy and brown on the outside? What kid could resist? And you can also appeal to your guests' parents with a menu that includes plenty of vegetables. Along with the Macaroni and Cheese, try serving carrot and celery sticks, corn chowder with assorted vegetables, ham rolls and birthday cake.

You'll love entertaining with this simple menu, because you can prepare everything ahead of time and just bake or reheat it before serving. The dishes adapt easily to feed a crowd of any size, and they require very little mealtime attention, which will free you for more pressing crowd-control duties. Because both the chowder and the casserole contain plenty of dairy products, you can do away with glasses of milk and treat your guests to fruit juice.

Macaroni and Cheese

2 pounds dried elbow macaroni · 1/2 cup butter · 1/2 cup flour
6 cups milk · 2 pounds Cheddar cheese, grated · salt and pepper to taste

Boil the macaroni in 2 batches until *al dente,* then drain and rinse. Set it aside.

Melt the butter over low heat, then gradually add the flour and stir until you have a smooth, golden paste.

Slowly pour in the milk, stirring constantly. Turn up the heat and continue mixing until the sauce just reaches the boiling point. Reduce the heat and allow the sauce to cook for a couple of minutes.

Add all but two cups of the grated cheese to the sauce, and cook until the cheese melts. Remove the sauce from the heat.

In one or two large bowls, toss the macaroni and sauce together. Grease two 9-by-13 inch baking pans, and pour half of the macaroni and cheese into each.

Sprinkle the remaining cheese evenly over the contents of the two pans. Bake at 350 degrees for half an hour before serving.

Serves 20

*T*here is no better way to celebrate something truly special than to host a formal dinner party.

Here's an elegant menu that's not meant for the fainthearted or inexperienced cook (though you can simplify the preparation by organizing a schedule that begins the day before the party): sorrel soup, fresh mozzarella and sundried tomatoes with basil and olive oil, fresh oysters on the half shell with shallot vinaigrette, Pappardelle with Duckling, julienne of carrots and zucchini, puree of butternut squash, wilted spinach salad with bleu cheese and hazlenuts and sachertorte.

Don't skimp on the ingredients to save money or your planning and hard work will come to naught. Choose the wines carefully, and be prepared to spend a little extra.

To do this elaborate menu justice, send out engraved invitations requesting black tie attire. Hire experienced staff to assist you in the kitchen and to do all the serving. Be sure to set the table with the silver required for each course and with separate crystal for water and each of the wines. And, of course, candlelight and flowers are de rigueur. Start out with a medium-bodied red wine such as a Rhone or Cabernet, then switch to a more powerful vintage such as a Chateauneuf-du-Pape or Barolo when you bring out the pappardelle. You may want to finish the meal off with a good Cognac.

Pappardelle with Duckling

For the noodles:

6 cups flour • 8 eggs • 2 teaspoons salt (optional)
2 tablespoons olive oil (optional)

For the sauce:

3 ducklings (2¼ pounds each) • 1/2 cup butter • 1 large onion, chopped
2 carrots, chopped • 2 sticks celery, chopped • 1/4 cup fresh parsley, chopped
2 teaspoons crumbled sage • 2 bay leaves • 1 cup dry white wine
1 cup stock • 4 ounces white truffles, sliced very thin
salt and pepper to taste

Make the pasta dough according to the instructions on page 26. Cut the pappardelle as directed on page 30. Cover and set aside.

Cut each duckling into about 6 pieces. Sauté the vegetables (but not the truffles) and herbs in the butter.

Place the duckling pieces in a large pot with the sautéed vegetables. You may have to distribute the ingredients between two pots. Simmer, covered, for 15 minutes.

Add the wine and stock. Cover and cook until the duckling is done.

Remove the duckling and allow it to cool. Strain the stock, season it with salt and pepper and return it to low heat.

Tear the duckling meat off the bones and cut it into bite-sized pieces. Return the meat to the stock pot and add the truffles.

While cooking the pappardelle, heat the sauce to serving temperature. Drain the noodles, place in individual serving bowls and top with the sauce. Serve with fresh ground black pepper.

Serves 12

*L*et the flavors of the Middle East transport you and your guests to the land of Scheherezade and The Arabian Nights with a menu that includes pita bread with humus, cold yogurt soup, Couscous with Lamb, carrot salad with raisins and dates, okra with tomatoes and baklava and Turkish coffee for dessert.

To make couscous, you need a couscoussier, a sealed steamer in which you cook pasta over a simmering stew. Because couscous will not cook properly unless the seal between the two sections of the steamer is perfectly tight, there is no satisfactory substitute for a couscoussier. This recipe, which serves 20, must be handled in 2 batches because of the small size of most couscoussiers. The harissa sauce, a traditional hot sauce, is available in Middle Eastern specialty shops. You can prepare everything on this menu in advance except the couscous, which is best when cooked soon before serving.

Heavy ceramic tableware, boldly patterned earth-toned linens, and dozens of flickering votive candles will create a luxurious atmosphere in which to enjoy this oriental menu. You might even provide your guests with cushions on the floor, where they can sit after selecting their food at a buffet.

Offer your guests a powerful red wine such as an Italian Barolo or an Australian Shiraz to accompany this meal.

Couscous with Lamb

1/2 cup olive oil · 4 pounds boneless lamb · 4 onions, sliced
1 teaspoon cayenne pepper · 1 teaspoon ground turmeric · 3 tablespoons ground cinnamon
1 teaspoon ground cloves · 1/2 teaspoon saffron · 4 cups uncooked couscous
5 carrots, sliced · 2 peeled turnips, cubed
8 tomatoes, chopped · 1 cup cooked chickpeas · 1 cup cooked fava beans
2 zucchinis, cubed · 1 green cabbage, sliced · 1 cup raisins · harissa sauce

In the bottom half of the couscoussier, cook the lamb and the onions in the olive oil until the meat begins to brown. Add the spices and enough water to cover the meat. Bring the stew to a boil, then reduce the heat, cover the pot and leave the stew to simmer for 45 minutes.

Moisten the couscous with cold water, fluffing it with your fingers to keep it from lumping. Put the couscous into the top half of the couscoussier.

When the meat has cooked for 45 minutes, add the vegetables to the stew. Place the top half of the couscoussier onto the bottom half. Cover and continue cooking for 30 minutes.

After the couscous has steamed for half an hour, remove the top half of the couscoussier and pour the couscous into a large bowl. Sprinkle it with cold water and use a fork or your fingers to break up lumps.

Return the couscous to the steamer, replace the steamer onto the stew pot and cover. Cook for 30 more minutes.

To serve, heap the couscous on a large platter and top it with the stew. Serve the harissa on the side (available in specialty food stores).

Serves 20

Nothing matches Italian food for enter- taining large gatherings of people. You can serve 25 people with this menu that's perfect for any celebration, from birth- days to winter holidays. Start with antipasto platters of marinated mussels, artichoke hearts, rolled anchovies, hearts of palm, feta cheese and greek olives, accompanied by plenty of Italian bread. Follow that with clams on the half shell. Then serve Veal Lasagne with Spinach Noodles and Egg- plant Lasagne. Although your guests might say they don't have room, serve them a salad after the main course, made of radicchio, romaine lettuce, sweet red pepper strips and mushrooms. End the meal with assorted Italian cookies and cappucino.

You can prepare everything on the menu— except the clams—hours or even a day or two in advance. The ingredients of the anti- pasto platters need merely to be removed from their packaging and arranged artfully, while the Italian cookies can be bought fresh from the bakery on the day of the party.

Set up one or two buffet tables, get out the chafing dishes and let your guests dig in. Buy several inexpensive jugs of red and white wine from Italy or California to serve with the meals, and keep plenty of sparkling mineral water on hand.

Veal Lasagne with Spinach Noodles

For the dough:

1 pound fresh spinach · 6 cups flour · 6 eggs · 1 teaspoon salt (optional)
2 tablespoons olive oil (optional)

For the filling:

2 tablespoons olive oil · 1 large onion, chopped · 2 cloves garlic, minced
2 pounds ground veal · 3/4 cup dry white wine · 5 cups tomato puree
1/4 cup fresh basil, chopped · 1/2 teaspoon cayenne pepper
2 cups grated Parmesan · 2 eggs, beaten · salt and pepper to taste
1 pound mozzarella, diced · 1/2 cup melted butter

Prepare the spinach pasta according to the directions on page 39. Cut the lasagne noodles as instructed on page 31. Parboil the lasagne in several batches for 1 minute, drain, and lay the noodles on a clean towel to dry.

Cook the onion and garlic in the olive oil until the onion turns transparent. Add the veal and sauté until the meat loses its pinkness.

Pour in the wine and cook until the alcohol evaporates. Add the tomato purée, basil, and cayenne and bring the sauce to a boil.

Reduce the heat and stir in the Parmesan cheese and beaten eggs. Season the sauce with salt and pepper, allow it to thicken, then remove it from the heat.

Grease two 9-by-13-inch baking pans and line the bottoms and sides with 1 layer of lasagne. Coat the lasagne with a generous portion of meat sauce and sprinkle some of the diced mozzarella on top. Continue layering the noodles, sauce and cheese until all are used up, finishing with a layer of lasagne.

Pour the melted butter over the contents of the baking pans. Bake the lasagne for 15 to 20 minutes at 350 degrees. Serve with grated Parmesan on the side.

Eggplant Lasagne

For the dough:

6 cups flour • 8 eggs • 1 tablespoon salt (optional)
2 tablespoons olive oil (optional) • grated Parmesan cheese

For the filling:

1/2 cup olive oil • 4 cloves garlic, minced • 1 dried red chili pepper • 2 large eggplants, diced
2 sweet yellow peppers, chopped • 3/4 pound mushrooms, sliced
4 pounds canned tomatoes, drained and chopped • 1 cup pitted, halved black olives
1/4 cup capers • 1/4 cup chopped fresh parsley • salt and pepper to taste
1/2 cup melted butter

Prepare the pasta dough according to the directions on page 26. Cut the lasagne noodles as instructed on page 31. Parboil the lasagne in several batches for 1 minute, drain, and lay the noodles on a clean towel to dry.

In the olive oil, sauté the garlic and crumbled chili pepper.

Add the eggplant, peppers and mushrooms and cook for about 5 minutes, stirring. Mix in the tomatoes and simmer until the eggplant is tender.

Add the black olives, capers, parsley, salt and pepper. Cook the sauce for another 10 minutes, adding water if it becomes too thick. Remove from the heat.

Grease two 9-by-13-inch baking pans and line the bottoms and sides with 1 layer of lasagne. Cover the lasagne with some of the vegetable sauce. Continue layering the noodles and sauce until both are used up, finishing with a layer of lasagne.

Pour the melted butter over the lasagne and bake the casseroles for 20 to 25 minutes at 350 degrees. Serve the lasagne with grated Parmesan cheese on the side.

These two lasagne recipes together serve 25

*C*hase away the February blahs by celebrating the Chinese New Year. Make
these two dishes, Cold Noodles with Sesame
Sauce and Ants on a Tree, which are perfectly suited to buffets for big crowds. Serve
them with cold hacked chicken with spicy
sauce, scallion pancakes, eggplant with garlic sauce, broccoli with straw mushrooms and
green tea ice cream and fortune cookies.

The vegetables and appetizers can be
made in advance or purchased from your
local Chinese restaurant and reheated at
party time. Make the meat sauce for Ants
on a Tree the day before the event—it will
actually taste better that way—and all you'll
have to do at the last minute is add the noodles. Prepare the dish in 3 batches to allow
for easier handling.

Find some paper lanterns and colorful
kites, set out chopsticks and oriental tableware, and treat your guests to an evening in
the Far East.

Serve Chinese beer and tea with the
meal, or, if you prefer wine, try Gewurztraminer, an aromatic white from Alsace.

Cold Noodles with Sesame Sauce

3 pounds Chinese egg noodles · 8 cloves garlic, pressed
2 tablespoons grated fresh ginger · 1 cup sesame paste (tahini)
1/3 cup soy sauce · 3 tablespoons rice wine · 1/4 cup sesame oil
1/3 cup red wine vinegar · 2 tablespoons sugar · 1 teaspoon chili oil or paste
2 cucumbers

Cook the noodles in 3 batches. Drain and rinse them under cold water and set
aside.

Combine all of the remaining ingredients except the cucumber in a food processor
or blender. Blend to a smooth sauce. Season to taste.

Peel and seed the cucumbers and cut them into very thin strips about 1½ inches
long.

Place the noodles, sauce and cucumbers in a large bowl and toss them before
serving.

Serves 25

Ants on a Tree

4 pounds dried bean threads (cellophane noodles) · 1/2 cup peanut oil
2 tablespoons grated fresh ginger · 12 cloves garlic, minced
2 dried hot chili peppers · 6 pounds lean ground pork
12 dried Chinese mushrooms, reconstituted and chopped · 12 scallions, chopped
1/2 cup soy sauce · 1/2 cup rice wine · 3 tablespoons corn starch
salt and pepper to taste

Soak the bean threads in hot water for 15 minutes. When they are soft, drain and rinse them with cold water. Shake off the excess water and set the noodles aside.

Prepare the meat sauce in 2 batches. Heat the peanut oil in a wok. When it just starts to smoke, add the ginger, garlic, and chili peppers. Stir-fry for 30 seconds.

Add the pork and stir-fry it until it has lost its pinkness. Mix in the mushrooms and scallions, then pour in the soy sauce and rice wine.

After a minute or so, gradually add as much of the cornstarch as you need to slightly thicken the mixture. If the sauce becomes too thick, add water. Season with salt and pepper.

Place equal quantities of the sauce in 4 separate pots. Stir 1/4 of the noodles into each and simmer the 4 batches over low heat for 5 to 10 minutes, covered. Serve in 2 or 3 large bowls or chafing dishes.

Serves 25

Sources

Balducci's
Mail-order Division
42-34 12th St.
Long Island City, NY 11101
(800) 225-3822 in New York State
specialty foods

Bloomingdale's
Petrossian Shop
1000 Third Ave.
New York, NY 10021
(212) 705-3176
caviar

C & K Importing Company
2771 West Pico Blvd.
Los Angeles, CA 90006
(213) 737-2970
Middle Eastern ingredients

Cardullo's Gourmet Shop
6 Brattle St.
Cambridge, MA
(617) 491-8888
preserved truffles

The Chef's Catalogue
3215 Commercial Ave.
Northbrook, IL 60062
(708) 480-9400
professional cookware

Community Kitchens Company
P.O. Box 2311
Baton Rouge, LA 70821
(800) 535-9901
professional cookware

Corti Brothers
5104 Arden Way
Carmichael, CA 95608-6005
(916) 483-6452
pasta and other Italian foods

Dean & Deluca
560 Broadway
New York, NY 10012
(212) 431-1691
(800) 221-7714
specialty foods

DeLaurenti
1435 First Ave.
Seattle, WA 98101
(206) 622-0141
specialty foods

DeWildt Imports, Inc.
30 Compton Way
Hamilton Square, NJ 08690
Indonesian spices

Figi's, Inc.
3200 South Maple Ave.
Marshfield, WI 54449
(715) 384-6101
smoked meats, cheeses

Fitz-Henri Fine Foods
2901 Bayview Ave.
Willowdale, ONT M2K 1E6
Canada
(416) 225-4175
gourmet specialties

Gaston Dupre, Inc.
7904 Hopi Place
Tampa, FL 33634
(813) 885-9445
all types of pasta

Susan Green's California Cuisine
3501 Taylor Dr.
Ukiah, CA 94582
(800) 753-8558

Hansen Caviar Company
93D South Railroad
Bergenfield, NY 07621
(201) 385-6221
imported and American caviars

Harrington's Ham Company, Inc.
Main Street
Richmonds, VT 05477
(802) 434-4444
*meats, cheeses, and other
gourmet items*

Harry and David
Bear Creek Orchards
Medford, OR 97501
(503) 776-2400
*fruits, smoked meats, and other
gourmet items*

The Honey Hollow
277A St. Jean Rd.
Pointe Claire, Quebec H4R 3J1
(514) 697-5153
specialty foods

House of Spices
76-17 Broadway
Jackson Heights, NY 11373
(718) 476-1577
spices

Japan Food Corporation
540 Forbes Boulevard
South San Francisco, CA 94080
(415) 244-6100
*Japanese and other Oriental
ingredients*

Kitchen Arts & Letters
1435 Lexington Ave.
New York, NY 10128
(212) 876-5550
cookbooks

Lambs Farm
P.O. Box 520
Libertyville, IL 60048
(708) 362-4636
*cheeses, breads, and other
gourmet items*

Maison E. H. Glass, Inc.
111 East 58th St.
New York, NY 10022
(212) 755-3316
specialty foods

Manganaro Foods
488 Ninth Ave.
New York, NY 10018
(212) 563-7748
Italian specialities

Marcel et Henri
415 Browning Way
South San Francisco, CA 94080
(415) 871-4230
pâtés and sausages

Market Square Food Company
1642 Richfield Ave.
Highland Park, IL 60035
(708) 831-2228
gourmet foods

Marshall Fields
Direct Response Center
P.O. Box 56
Minneapolis, MN 55440
(800) 292-2450
specialty foods and cookware

Neiman Marcus
P.O. Box 2968
Dallas, TX 75221
(800) 634-6267
specialty foods and cookware

Norm Thompson Outfitters, Inc.
P.O. Box 3999
Portland, OR 97229
(800) 547-1160
*smoked salmon, cheeses, and other
gourmet items*

Nueske Hillcrest Farm Meats
R.R. 2
Witenberg, WI 54499
(800) 382-2266
hams, bacon, and sausages

Paprikas Weiss Gourmet Shop
1572 Second Ave.
New York, NY 10028
(212) 288-6117
Eastern European specialties

Sutton Place Gourmet
3201 New Mexico Ave. NW
Washington, D.C. 20016
(202) 363-5800
fresh and preserved truffles

Taylor Herb Gardens, Inc.
1535 Lone Oak Rd.
Vista, CA 92084
(619) 727-3485
fresh herbs

Todaro Bros.
Mail-order Department
555 Second Ave.
New York, NY 10016
(212) 532-0633
Italian specialty foods

Totem Smokehouse
1906 Pike Place
Seattle, WA 98101
(800) 9 SALMON
smoked salmon

Uwajimaya
P.O. Box 3003
Seattle, WA 98114
(206) 624-6248
Japanese and Chinese foods

Williams-Sonoma
Mail Order Department
P.O. Box 7456
San Francisco, CA 94210-7456
(800) 541-2233
kitchen supplies

Zabar's

2245 Broadway
New York, NY 10024
(212) 787-2000
specialty foods and cookware

Index

Additional photographs: © Simon Feldman/Envision p 14, © Michael Grand p 38a, © Steven Mark Needham/Envision p 38b, © Michael Grand p 48, © Michael Grand p 63, © Burke/Triolo p 67, © Felicia Martinez/PhotoEdit p 71, © Steven Mark Needham/Envision p 74, Courtesy Williams-Sonoma p 90, © Felicia Martinez/PhotoEdit p 92b, © Michael Grand p 113.

Illustrations by Judy L. Morgan

有一年春天，堂姐接我和弟弟去奶奶家。

奶奶家好远，我们坐了整整一天的绿皮火车，

还坐了好几个小时的摆渡船。

奶奶家在长江中的一个洲上。

那是我头一次看到长江。

当听到有人指着江里的一条条大鱼喊

"江猪！江猪！"时，

我还奇怪，明明是鱼，怎么叫猪呢？

后来等我长大了，才知道江猪就是江豚。

这都是五十多年前的事情了。

那一年，我六岁。

弟弟四岁。

图书在版编目（ＣＩＰ）数据

公鸡的唾沫 / 彭懿文；王祖民图. -- 广州：
新世纪出版社, 2019.7
ISBN 978-7-5583-0822-2

Ⅰ.①公… Ⅱ.①彭… ②王… Ⅲ.①儿童故事
－图画故事－中国－当代 Ⅳ.①I287.8

中国版本图书馆CIP数据核字(2019)第177867号

GONGJI DE TUOMO

蒲蒲兰绘本馆 公鸡的唾沫

彭懿 文　王祖民 图

出 版 人：姚丹林
责任编辑：李世文　庄淳楦
责任技编：陈静娴
特约编辑：高 媛 马皓月

出版发行：新世纪出版社
（510102 广州市大沙头四马路10号）
经销：新华书店
印刷：鸿博昊天科技有限公司
规格：889mm×1194mm
开本：12
印张：4.5
字数：56千
版次：2019年11月第1版
印次：2019年11月第1次印刷
定价：49.80元

公鸡的唾沫

彭懿 文　王祖民 图

SPM

南方出版传媒

新世纪出版社

·广州·

下了船，堂哥已经推着一辆独轮车在等我们了。
从码头到奶奶家，还有好几里路要走。
没有大马路，全是难走的田间小路。

弟弟吵着闹着要坐独轮车，堂哥拗不过他，只好把他抱了上去。
穿过一片稻田时，可能是田埂太烂了，堂哥脚下一滑，
车身歪了一下，弟弟滚到了稻田里。等堂哥把他捞出来的时候，
他已经变成了一条黑不溜秋的小"泥鳅"。

奶奶的村子很小，只有十几户人家。
堂姐说，村子里的人都是亲戚，
都姓一个姓，都姓杨。

奶奶和爷爷已经等在村口了。

妈妈说，我出生的时候，

奶奶和爷爷来看过我。

不过我早忘了他们的模样。

奶奶矮矮的，

穿着一件我从没见过的大襟褂。

爷爷高高的，

穿着一条我从没见过的缅裆裤。

奶奶没有抱我，爷爷也没有，

他们一起拉住了弟弟的手。

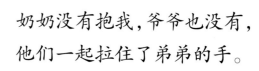

奶奶家不是草房，是瓦房，
不过墙是泥土墙，屋子里的地，
也是泥土地。

奶奶问我要不要跟她一起睡觉，我说不要。
一是我跟她亲不起来，
二是她睡的那张雕花大木床太高了，
还要踩着一条长长的踏板，才能爬上去。
弟弟睡在奶奶身边。
我睡在墙边一个长长的柜子上。
那天晚上，我躲在被窝里偷偷地哭了，
我想爸爸妈妈，我想回家。

第二天早上起来一看，奶奶已经在推磨磨米了。

"奶奶今天给我们包团子吃！"弟弟说。

眼看着，那盆泡了一夜的糯米就被磨成了白色的米浆。

接着，奶奶用一块干净的白布把它们兜住。

水"哗哗"地流了出来，留在布里头的，就是一块块的水磨粉了。

奶奶会包两种团子。

一种是咸的秧草菜团子，一种是甜的水晶芝麻团子。

奶奶先把水磨粉在手上捏成一个团子，

然后用指头在中间捅一个大洞，让我们帮她把馅儿塞进去。

用来煮团子的，是一口黑乎乎的大铁锅。
弟弟抢着烧火，不停往灶里添稻草，
我负责往锅里扔团子。
等水"咕嘟咕嘟"地烧开时，
一个个团子浮了上来。
奶奶包的团子特别大，
足足有鹅蛋那么大。

"吃吃吃!""吃吃吃!"

奶奶说完爷爷说,爷爷说完奶奶说。

可团子实在是太大了,我只吃了一个秧草菜团子,

就再也吃不下去了。

弟弟厉害,连吃了两个水晶芝麻团子。

不过等他吃完,肚子就鼓得像蝈蝈一样大了。

这天夜里，我去撒尿时，
被地上一个尖溜溜的东西绊了一跤。
第二天早上爬起来一看，
地面上竟然冒出来了一根竹笋！
爷爷拿来一把铲子，要把它挖掉，
可是弟弟死活不让挖，
他说他要看着它长成一根高高的竹子。
太稀奇了，屋子里竟会长竹笋。

这根竹笋长得好快，
晚上躺在被窝里仔细听，
都能听到它"噌——噌——"的拔节声。
"再不吃，它就老了，就不好吃了。"
两天后，趁弟弟不在家，
奶奶还是把它挖了出来，
烧了一盘竹笋红烧肉。
奶奶说，竹笋最配的就是红烧肉。

这里家家户户的屋后都有一口塘，一片竹林。
塘有一个篮球场那么大，塘里的水很清，
清得看得见小鱼和小虾。
人们不但喝塘里的水，还在塘里洗菜、淘米、洗衣服。
奶奶说："塘里的水是活水，塘连着河，河连着江，
干净着哪！"

奶奶家有两个大木盆，屋里一个，屋外一个。屋里那个，是澡盆。
屋外那个，是采菱用的，叫菱盆。澡盆和菱盆的样子不一样，
澡盆是圆的，菱盆是椭圆形的，长长的，就像一粒大豌豆。
奶奶就坐在菱盆里采菱。塘里的菱太多了，
简直就像一个绿色的盖子，几乎把整个塘都盖住了。
不过，浮在水面上的不是菱，是菱的叶子，菱长在它们的根上。

菱盆里有一把小簸箕，
因为水会从木缝里渗进来，
要是不把它们舀出去，
菱盆就会沉掉。

我和奶奶都喜欢吃菱。

刚煮出来的嫩菱，水灵灵的、热乎乎的，
用牙一咬，壳就裂开了。里面的肉，白白胖胖的，
又甜又脆，每次我和奶奶都能吃满满一大盆。

弟弟不喜欢吃菱，他说菱滑溜溜的，吃上去像鼻涕虫。

还有一个人，也不喜欢吃菱。这个人就是爷爷。

当他听到弟弟这么说时，就把弟弟抱到自己的大腿上，

开心地说："这才是我的大孙子！"

乡下好玩的事情太多。

不过最好玩的事情，要数下雨天。

村子里的路，全是土路。要是连着下上一天的雨，

村子里的路就会变成一片烂泥塘。

堂哥堂姐他们去邻居家串门，全都要踩高跷。

路上来来往往的人，都踩着高跷，就好像在表演杂技一样。

我和弟弟最喜欢去村里的杂货店打酱油。
杂货店的婶婶总是一边"咿呀咿呀"地哄着身后的小毛头，
一边从一个大木桶里舀出一勺酱油，顺着漏斗，
慢慢地倒进酱油瓶里。
她每次都会用牛皮纸包一袋方片糕，
送给我们作礼物。

夏天的傍晚，我们会把装着萤火虫的瓶子挂到
院子里的梨树上，当灯照亮。
树下有一张竹床，我和弟弟躺在上面。
奶奶就坐在我们的身边，用一把大蒲扇帮我们赶蚊子。

爷爷也会搬一把竹椅凑过来，给我们讲故事。
"你爸爸小时候呀，就喜欢下河游泳，怎么说都不听。
没办法，我就每天早上在他的脚底板用毛笔写上一个字，
然后让你奶奶用布把他的脚包上。
晚上回来检查，要是那个字没了，被水洗掉了，
就说明他又下河游泳了，我就要狠狠地揍他一顿……"

有天半夜，我不知道是被什么虫子咬醒了，
浑身痒得要命。"咔嚓咔嚓咔嚓"，我搔个不停。
奶奶听到了，连忙下床，举起煤油灯一照，
叫了起来："哎呀，你的小胳膊都被抓烂了！"
奶奶倒了一小碟做豆腐的卤水，
在我的胳膊上轻轻地涂了起来。
虽然有点蜇，不过好多了。

可能是我的头垂得太低了，有一束头发掉到了煤油灯里，
"嗤啦"一下，头发被烧着了。
还好奶奶眼疾手快，用手一撸，
把我头发上的火撸灭了。

等到田里的稻子黄了的时候，田里的螃蟹也长大了。

一个个圆滚滚的，有小拳头那么大。人一走过来，

它们就会横着身子，飞快地逃回到田埂上的那些小洞洞里。

堂哥说，那些扁的洞，是螃蟹的洞；圆的，是黄鳝和小蛇的洞。

我不敢掏那些螃蟹洞，怕被它们的大钳子夹手。

弟弟敢，他好像什么都不怕。

每天弟弟都能抓到好多只螃蟹，竹篓子都装不下。

我和弟弟最喜欢看爷爷吃螃蟹。

爷爷太会吃螃蟹了，一只螃蟹吃完，摆在桌子上，

还是一只螃蟹，看上去就好像没有吃过一样。

我看得正起劲儿，突然听到弟弟这样问爷爷：

"爷爷，你都这么老了，你什么时候死啊？"

爷爷没有生气，只是"呵呵"地笑着，一个劲儿地摇晃着脑袋：

"童言无忌，童言无忌……"这四个字，怎么听都像是咒语。

果然，第二天弟弟"童言无忌"的报应就来了。
弟弟一个人去屋后的竹林里捉蚂蚱喂鸡，
脸被马蜂蜇了一下，一路尖叫着跑了回来。

奶奶一把抓过醋瓶子，
把醋倒在自己的手上，
往弟弟脸上使劲儿抹，
然后又冲到杂货店，
问婶婶要来了一壶小毛头的尿。
"来，快用这壶尿洗个脸！"

见奶奶要朝自己的脸上浇尿，弟弟哪肯啊，
他捂着肿成一条线的眼睛就逃出去了。
爷爷抱着一只大公鸡，从后面追了上去。
"等等！再抹点公鸡的唾沫！"
尽管奶奶后来解释说小毛头的尿是民间秘方，
但弟弟还是三天没跟她睡觉。

转眼就到了秋天。

有一天，我听到爷爷跟奶奶商量说："要不，就早点起塘吧，让孩子们尝尝塘里的大鱼。"

后来我才知道，起塘就是把塘里的水抽干，清淤捉鱼。

堂哥和好多大哥哥在塘边踩了好几天的水车，才把塘里的水抽干。那时没有电，没有抽水机，全靠水车。

除了春节，起塘，算是村里最重要的一个节日了。

起塘那天，几乎村里所有的男女老少都来帮忙下塘捉鱼。

"来，看看你长胖了几斤？"
爷爷拿来一个竹篮，让弟弟坐到里面，
然后他用一根大杆秤的钩子钩住篮子，
抓住提绳往上一拎，没拎动。
于是，爷爷找来一根竹扁担，从提绳里穿过去，
又叫来奶奶，两个人用肩膀把扁担扛了起来。
弟弟整整重了三斤。我想起来了，
从前爸爸说过，他们那边都是这样称小孩的。
爷爷问我要不要称，我连忙摇头，
我又不是鱼，我才不要被人扛着称呢！

我们回家前一天的晚上。奶奶拎来一篮子鸡蛋，又抱来一捆晒干的笋壳，
开始扎起鸡蛋来。那时，乡下最珍贵的东西就是鸡蛋了。
奶奶把鸡蛋一只一只地放到笋壳里。一片笋壳，正好放五只鸡蛋。
然后，奶奶把另外一片笋壳盖在上面，用绳子把每一只鸡蛋都扎牢。
扎好的笋壳，看上去就像一节节的莲藕。我一觉醒来，
看到奶奶还在煤油灯下扎鸡蛋。那天晚上，我睡在了奶奶的床上。

我们回家那天，
全村每家人都拎着一篮子鸡蛋，来给我们送行。
鸡蛋太多了，堂哥的独轮车根本就装不下。

我们走出很远了，我回头看，
奶奶和爷爷还没有离去，还在冲我们挥手。

作者介绍　彭懿

1958 年出生于沈阳。童话幻想小说及绘本作家。

他父亲的故乡在本溪张其寨村，五岁时，他曾跟奶奶回去过一趟，不过除了坐绿皮火车的记忆，他什么印象也没留下。1976 年高中毕业，他插过队，在新民小梁山当过一年的知青，小梁山最出名的是小梁山西瓜，不过，他一个西瓜也没吃着，整天赶着小毛驴车往田里拉肥料，种玉米……

因为他喜欢写童话，后来稀里糊涂地被辽宁省地震局借去，写了一本名叫《在征服地震的道路上》的科普书的半本书稿，不过这本书出版时，人家没有署他的名，只是在后记中提到他写了部分初稿。一气之下，1977 年他考上了复旦大学生物系，立志毕业之后当一名科普作家，可是在出版了《西天目山捕虫记》《小小蚂蚁国》之后，他发现还是写童话更好玩，于是他成了一个特好玩的童话作家。

绘者介绍　王祖民

1949 年出生于南京。画家。

1968 年初中毕业，他坐了一夜的长江渡轮，然后又换大木船，到江心沙农场当知青。这是一座离崇明很近的岛，它四面环水，连个码头都没有。他还记得他当时是搭跳板上的岸。起初，他跟当地人一起放牛，因为会画画，后来被农场抽去在墙上画宣传画。他还当过农场子弟学校的美术老师，从一年级教到初三。因为当地缺医少药，他又被抽去做赤脚医生……六年以后，他被推荐上大学，本来是去医学院学医的，结果被人调包，上了美术学院，阴差阳错成了一名获奖无数的画家。

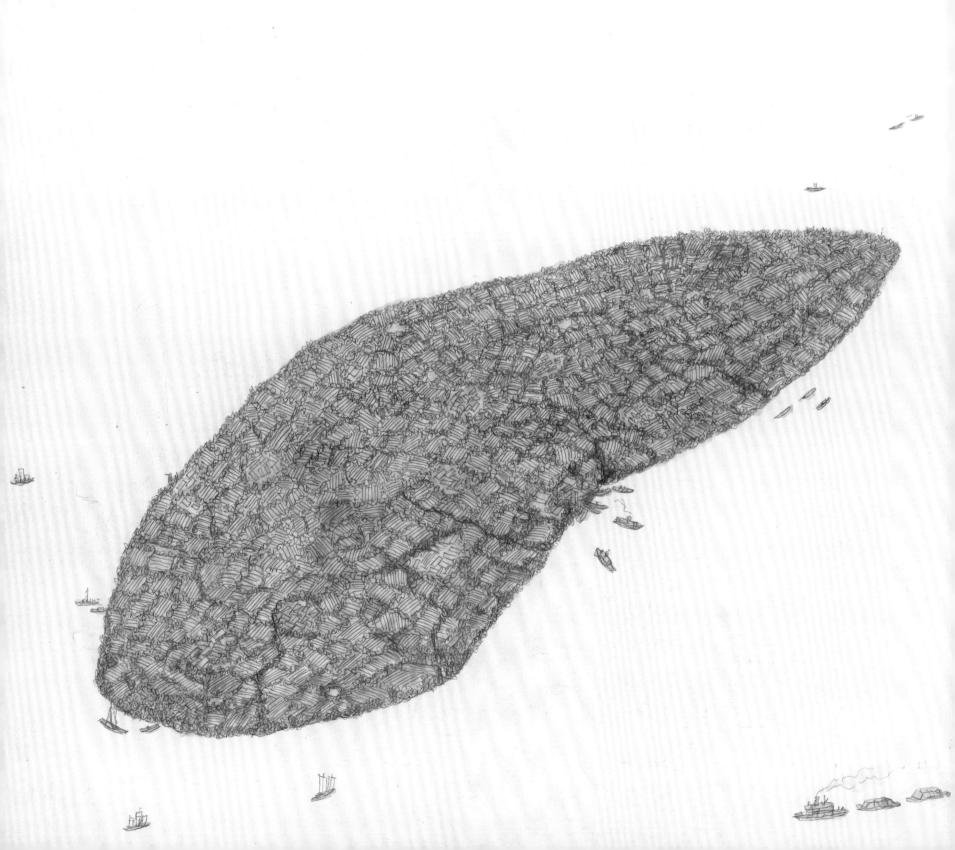